Maria Jolas,
Woman of Action

Maria Jolas, Woman of Action

A Memoir and Other Writings

Edited by Mary Ann Caws

University of South Carolina Press

© 2004 University of South Carolina

Published in Columbia, South Carolina, by the
University of South Carolina Press

Manufactured in the United States of America

08 07 06 05 04 5 4 3 2 1

Library of Congress Cataloging-in-Publication Data

Jolas, M.
  Maria Jolas, woman of action : a memoir and other writings / edited by Mary Ann
Caws.
    p. cm.
  Includes index.
  ISBN 1-57003-550-4 (alk. paper)
  1. Jolas, M. 2. Translators—France—Biography. I. Caws, Mary Ann. II. Title.
  P306.92.J65A3 2004
  418'.02'092—dc22

2004007736

Photographs and writings of Maria Jolas used by permission of Betsy Jolas. The editor
expresses her gratitude to the Beinecke Rare Book and Manuscript Library, Yale University, for use of their archives on Maria Jolas.

Contents

Illustrations

Introduction

A survivor of the heroic generation, they said of her. In the *Paris Review,* she was once called, somewhat to her discomfort, "The Leading Lady of Paris Literati of the Thirties." Maria Jolas, with her usual modesty, crossed out this description, replacing it with this one: "merely the close collaborator—shall we say Editorial Assistant—to my husband Eugene Jolas, founder and editor of the magazine *transition.*" She was not even listed on the masthead of this highly important publication, which ran from 1927 to 1938, publishing—often for the first time —many writers essential to our understanding of modernism: Samuel Beckett, James Joyce, Gertrude Stein, and many others.

It was the crucial role of Maria Jolas in *transition* and in modernism in general that encouraged me initially in my enthusiasm for publishing the memoir she had carefully prepared for publication—and which I have therefore treated with a very light hand. *Man from Babel,* Eugene Jolas's autobiography (edited, annotated, and introduced by Andreas Kramer and Rainer Rumold, New Haven: Yale University Press, 1998), does much to illuminate the life of the Jolas family and their literary enterprises. Dougald McMillan's careful study of the history of the journal, *transition: The History of a Literary Era, 1927–38* (London: Calder and Boyars; New York: G. Braziller, 1976), is invaluable.

This memoir and its various associated journal drafts trace Maria's childhood in Louisville, Kentucky, with the McDonald family, her studies to become a singer, her travel to Berlin for her music studies, her return to the United States at the outset of World War I, and her departure for Paris after the war to continue her voice lessons with her New York teacher. It speaks of her meeting Eugene Jolas through his brother, the pianist Jacques Jolas, and their marriage in January 1926. It traces the birth of their two daughters, Betsy, the celebrated composer, and Marie Christine (Tina), the anthropologist and translator. It deals with the founding and history of *transition,* with the Jolas's renting of what was eventually to be Charles de Gaulle's house in Colombey-les-Deux-Eglises, and with Maria's founding of l'Ecole Bilingue, which operated in Neuilly from 1932 to 1938 and then outside of St. Gérand-le Puy from 1939 to 1940. It recounts Maria's departure for the United States with Betsy and Tina (Eugene having already departed) and their experiences here (including Maria's radio talks and political activities) before Maria's return to Paris in February 1946, when she was the public relations officer for the American Aid to France. Tina returned to France in the fall of 1945, Betsy in the summer of 1946. Both daughters married Frenchmen, and Maria became a grandmother several times over.

She was a protestor against the war in Vietnam, making many political speeches and becoming a familiar figure on the streets of the Left Bank. Many of us knew of her first as the tireless friend of James Joyce, whose family she helped over and over, whose daughter, Lucia, she kept up with, whose proofs she read, and whose possessions she managed to rescue after the war. Then we knew her as the superb translator of the works of Gaston Bachelard and of Nathalie Sarraute, perhaps her best friend, because of whom she lived in the village of Chérence, about an hour from Paris. As for my personal acquaintance with Maria Jolas, I knew her through my friendship with her daughter Tina, with whom I translated the poetry of René Char—but I had always been greatly impressed by Maria's reputation and endurance as a translator (I had myself given up translating Bachelard at the very thought of having to do more than five volumes). Any time spent with her was in itself a powerful experience—in fact, unforgettable.

Herbert Lottman describes her, in his piece for the *New York Times* of March 22, 1970, called "One of the Quiet Ones," as "this ever-young neighbor" whose "fervor sweeps all the scenery off the stage. . . . Indisputably, Maria Jolas is part of Paris, part of a legend we nourish when we walk down the Rue Monsieur-le-Prince and look into a restaurant Joyce used to frequent." He quotes one of Joyce's friends to describe Maria as "tall, laughing-eyed, radiating mingled good humor and efficiency."

Irving Marder, in the *International Herald Tribune* of May 12, 1972, describes an interview with "Maria Jolas, the Militant." "The woman who opened the door," he wrote, "might have stepped out of one of those huge Delacroix paintings—a heroic figure of Liberty, Freedom, and/or Justice. Tall and handsome with a mass of well-groomed white hair, she gives an impression of radiant good health and vitality." That description, I think, she would have preferred to the description one of the "quiet ones."

The heroic figure is, as I read her, the person who comes out so clearly in these pages—in her memoir, but also in the various radio addresses and the letters and scraps of journal, some of which I have included here, translating them from the French when necessary. I have thought them an integral part of Maria's vivid life as she recounts it so inimitably. The memoir itself is augmented by her memories, written when she was past eighty, of the founding of the school and of the war years, found in sketch form.

The essential legacy of Maria Jolas has often been effaced behind that of her colorful husband and their famous friends, Joyce in particular. I wanted her to have her own voice, her own expression, and her own story.

Included here is the dateline Maria Jolas has given of her own life, and the outline of the way in which she would have wanted to publish her entire memoir. As it was actually written out full length, when she was eighty, it ceases with the family's renting of a house in Colombey-les-Deux-Eglises. These are the years of the founding of the journal *transition*—of which a photograph of the first issue's cover page is included here. Directly following the last word of the fully typed out memoir, which is the word *transition,* and excerpts from her journal, I have placed the famous manifesto called "The Revolution of the Word," dating from 1929. After that, her memoir is hand-written.

I have followed her wishes, inserted the material she wished inserted, including the dates and places mentioned, and placed the chapters as she had thought best. I have employed italics for the underlined foreign expressions and emphasized words in the typescript, and I have standardized the use of underlining for titles. I have supplied the chapter titles; otherwise I have left the memoir untouched, as I have the radio addresses and the letters from Paris to her husband.

Given the detailed interest of Maria Jolas's documentary reporting on her life and times, including her radio addresses while in the United States; her lectures to French and American groups about folklore, various exhibitions, and the Cantine La Marseillaise; her journals from Paris and New York; her letters to her husband while she was in Paris and he in Germany; her recounting of her continuing help to the Joyce family; and her recollections of the founding and continuing of l'Ecole Bilingue in Neuilly and then in St.-Gérand, I have thought it best to attach the majority of these texts as an entirety. When they are translated from the French or excerpted, I have noted that. Most of these documents, some of them quite lengthy, fall between the years 1940 and 1946 (that is, from wartime, and then her time back in the United States), whereas the sketch of her life subsequently (1952–1970, for example) is very short.

The pictures I have chosen seemed to me appropriate for the texts, including pictures of Maria in her childhood in Kentucky; of Eugene; of the Jolas family; of the Cantine La Marseillaise; of Pierre Vidal-Naquet, Maria's good friend and a close companion to the participants in the antiwar movement at the time of the conflict in Vietnam; of Maria participating in that movement; and several of James Joyce, including one with the surrealist writer Philippe Soupault, whose texts Maria had translated for *transition.*

The book concludes with the "End–dream," a term Maria borrows from her friend Samuel Beckett. The title lacks nostalgia, she says, but—and I hope it is true for the reader—has a certain hope and a great deal of warmth.

I want to thank in particular the composer Betsy Jolas for her constant encouragement, Vincent Giroud of the Beinecke Library, and Barry Blose of the University of South Carolina Press for his sustaining of this project over the years it has taken. I dedicate this work to Maria's daughters, Tina and Betsy, and their children.

Maria Jolas,
Woman of Action

Dateline, by Maria Jolas

Part I   1895–1915

Louisville, Kentucky	Childhood, schooling, church (traditional liberal Jeffersonian southern upbringing); large family, neither rich nor poor; Episcopal Church; personal freedom Summers in Michigan, Virginia, Tennessee Piano, church choir, guitar, Wednesday night music club
New York	Boarding school, piano lessons 1910–1912 opera, concerts Music student, singing 1913
Berlin	Music student, boarded with a friend of my parents 1913–1914 (June) Lilli Lehmann, Elena Gerhart, Arthur Nikisch, expressionists, etc. *First World War*

Part II   1915–1926

Louisville, on visits	
New York	Music student, jobs as telegraph operator, clerk at Charles Scribners', etc.; some Greenwich Village incursions
Paris, 1919	Followed singing teacher; music student Met Georges Duthuit, Brancusi, Zadkine; Montparnasse: Dôme, Rotonde, etc. Les Six. Stravinsky

1924	Visiting in Louisville, where my father died of a stroke in June; left me financially independent (later made <u>transition</u>, then my school possible)
1925	Met Eugene Jolas, who was writing a weekly literary column for the <u>Chicago Tribune</u>; we went together to a PEN Club affair, where we were introduced to Joyce. Galsworthy presided.

Part III   1926–1946

New York, January 1926	Marriage, back parlor of St. Patrick's Cathedral
New Orleans, February to May 1926	Life in the French Quarter Met Sherwood Anderson Met Edmund Wilson, trip up the *Bayoux* together
return to Paris, June 1926	Betsy's birth Preparation for <u>transition</u> (between 1927 and 1939 we brought out 27 issues of <u>transition</u>—contact with many writers and artists)
Colombey-les-Deux-Eglises, April 1927–October 1929	Beginning of 12 year friendship with Joyce Tina's birth, 1929
visit to U.S. 1928, Louisville and New York	Try to sell surrealist anthology; no buyers
Paris, 1931	Georgia's birth and early death
Neuilly	L'Ecole Bilingue, 1932–1940
Louisville, 1934	Mother's illness and death in 1935
Feldkirch and Utelle vacations	Matisse, Farandoles
Munich, 1938	Visit of Siqueiros
Switzerland, August 1939	
La Baule, August 1939	Boarding houses, valises
Paris *September 1939*	Lutetia—blackout Moved school, tangled with Pétainist proprietors

St. Gérand, Hôtel de la Paix	Christmas dinner, pains, dance
January 1940	The last
February 2nd	School problems, Sundays at La Chapelle, tea and radio, Goethe material, my dinners at hotel
March	Comments on phoney war
Easter	Children gone, Beckett, music, lying in the grass
April	Hôtel du Beaujolais; cinemas, walks, my weekly dinners
	Request for rights to publish in Chile
	Visit to Moulins, à propos of Lucia
La Chapelle, June 17	Arrival at La Chapelle, then Ragettly apartment; as Germans came through village, letter about Giorgio, "destroy immediately" Radio
July 1	Hôtel du Commerce, separate dining-room, depression routine
	Up late, listening to radio; transatlantic
	Visits to consulates in Vichy, walks with Leon, log by roadside, Ireland
	My trip to Marseille, visits to Vichy, Murphy, letters about Lucia
	Distress over anti-Semitism, over wine rulings
August 28	My departure, his accompanying me, insisted on carrying valises, waving blindly on platform
	My efforts to obtain money in America; letters about Lucia; lists of books and portraits
	World War II
New York, 1940–1946	I left for U.S. in September 1940; he left for Zurich in December, died there January 1941.
	I direct Cantine La Marseillaise (Free French)
	Gene leaves for Europe 1943, in PSY services
New York, 1944–1945	I work for the Office of War Information
	Liberation of Paris—All night street dancing: Marlene Dietrich, Jean Gabin, and hundreds of others
	Our house on East 74th Street: French artists and intellectuals in New York, especially

	André Masson and fmily. André du Bouchet, Jean Wahl, André Breton, Calder, etc.
Paris, February 1946	I return to Paris as Public Relations officer for the American Aid to France (private organization). Tina had left in November with the Duthuits, and Gene was still in Germany. Betsy finished her year at Bennington College.

Part IV   1946–1975

Postwar Paris	Food and housing shortages; Gene still serving in Germany; constant moves. (From family and intellectual activity, then the solitary years—children married, husband dead—to years of parallel political and literary activities that, almost before I knew it, confronted me with my 80th birthday)
1947	First Royaumont decade under Jean Wahl Visits to Nora Joyce in Zurich; Lucia, in Ivry
1948	transition '48 with Duthuit. Work with Beckett (translating); Betsy at the Conservatoire; Tina passing bac at Sévigné; Monique Roman (Lévi-Strauss) living with us; I visit Gene in Munich with Betsy and Tina
1949	I fetch and sort Joyce material Betsy and Tina marry, grandchildren
Paris, 1949	Joyce exhibition at La Hune, Sylvia Beach
Chérence, 1950	Natascha (Nathalie Sarraute)
1951	Gene's illness
1952	Gene's death in Paris
1952–1964	Moved 5 times Translating Sarraute, Bachelard, Garcilaso, Vidal-Naquet, Jaulin, et al; cafés, Collège Philosophique, grandchildren
1964	Visiting U.S. with Nathalie Sarraute

1965	Anti-Vietnam war; PACS, FAIRI, war crimes; deserters; American movement (Chomsky, Dellinger, Hayden, Fonda, Ira Morris, Raskin, Barnett, Falk, etc.); English movement; Stockholm; Indochinese friends
1968	"Evénements"
1973	80th birthday
Paris, 1975	Joyce symposium V

Part V   Identity

"Wasp?" Not quite; the Cavaliers were not Puritans, were even inclined to be frivolous and lazy

"Bourgeois?" I would like to think not; privileged, however, in many ways? What useful spiritual legacy for my descendants?

Preface to the Autobiography, by Maria Jolas

Although I have called this book an autobiography, it will not contain an account of my own most intimate experiences. So what I shall try to tell will be the story of a life, my own, which having begun in the receding resentments of a localized, fratricidal conflict, passed unscathed—when so many fell!—through the long period of international conflicts, and is now confronted with the spectacle of violence and global "brinkmanship" that a few neanderthal usurpers of power are offering a helpless, bemused world.

What did I do or leave undone? What did my generation do or leave undone to make this tragic escalation possible in the space of one life?

The Autobiography

"Carry me along, Taddy, like you done through the toy fair." The words are James Joyce's, but the experience was mine, drawn from the well of distant recall in the course of a dinner-table discussion: how far back can memory reach?

It was night, we were walking along the acetylene-lighted, dusty "midway" of the Jefferson County Fair, on the outskirts of Louisville Kentucky. I was perched on my tall young father's broad shoulders, my legs dangling onto his chest, hands clasping his head. Was Mother with us? Were there two older children walking beside us? Was there a younger sister or a new baby at home? Perhaps, indeed, probably, but I have no recollection of their existence at that time. Dazzled by the lights, the noisy crowds, the garish booths lining each side of the road, with the broad night sky above and, beneath me, my father's safe shoulders, I was unaware of everything but my own bliss. Joyce used my "ride" in a minor key, at the very end of Finnegans Wake, when the approach of night was leading him to seek again the warmest, surest haven he had known, that of his own father, his "mad-feary" father's unswerving love.

Today, with my eightieth birthday well behind me, other happy things float up to the surface. All-pervading is the colour red: the short red-brick walk, freshly reddened every Saturday, that led from the sidewalk across the lawn to the front door; the fragrant, deep-red roses on the bush that bordered this walk; the large sprawling red buildings that composed the Manual Training School, corner Brook and Oak Streets, opposite the red brick house in which, in 1893 —the year of what was termed "the great panic"—I was born. As a big girl, shall we say some ten to twelve years old, I knew that if, for sentimental reasons, you wanted the "Manual" team to win the football match, you wore a white chrysanthemum pinned to your coat, from which hung to your skirt hem, two long red satin streamers.

There were other colours: deep blue Concord grapes hanging from the "grape barber" that arched over the kitchen walk; the dark shade cast on the mossy bricks by the grape leaves; the bright pink of a peach-tree in bloom; the iridescent glow of the corner arc-light underneath which, on summer evenings, we ran and shouted after the street-cars that screeched around the corner. In early spring, in a friendly neighbour's back-yard, if you knew where to look, there were, too, tiny white and pale yellow violets.

These neighbours, a middle-aged, childless couple named Pirtle, had the rare gift of communicating normally and as between equals with young children. They neither scolded nor patronized, and unlike the jocular grocer across the way, they never teased. Escape from what I already sensed to be a somewhat crowded, autocratically run base to the intelligent serenity of "the Pirtles," a serenity I still identify with the white and yellow violets in the damp corner of their back-yard, had a calming effect on the frustrations that accompanied my position of "middle" child. One might ask: who composed the crowd? Who were the autocrats? Actually, the crowd was my own nuclear family: two parents and then three girls and two boys, with a period of ten years between the eldest and the youngest. A medium-sized family, really, when one recalls that my paternal grandfather had eighteen children, divided equally between two wives. However, if we add to the nuclearites a young uncle, Mother's brother William Carr, and a grandmother, Mrs. Cornelia Peake McDonald, I am inclined to think that my impression of being pressed for breathing space, at least the kind I needed, may not have been entirely unfounded. For the house was surely not very large.

The autocrats, as was typical of the time in the southern United States, were women: two white, Mother and Grandmother, and one black, Viney, whose terrorist rule covered not only the kitchen and pantry, which was her rightful domain, but also the cellar and entire back-yard, to which I was usually relegated. I did make an occasional escape, regularly sanctioned however by spanking— Mother preferred the slipper—and at times by a more distressing form of punishment (how I wept!) which consisted in being sent to bed without supper, while out-of-doors, children played and shouted under the arc-light, without me. The slipper, I believe, was for less serious misdemeanors, and there was no uncertainty as to who would wield it; Father never touched any of us otherwise than affectionately.

The senior autocrat, his mother, let the flak from her papal bulls fall as it would on young and old, male and female, black and white alike. She knew better, even than "that vulgarian Noah Webster"—correct pronunciation and spelling were subjects of frequent controversy—she held the tables of the law in her hand, no deviation would be tolerated. Indeed I recall a sudden sense of weightless terror when one day, during family prayers, after she had directed a sharp reprimand at us kneeling miscreants, I heard Father say firmly: "Mother, you raised your children as you thought best, I shall do the same with mine." No, the house did not come a-tumbling down like the walls of Jericho, but I asked myself why this had not happened. Here were Zeus and Athena in disagreement before us and, worse still, about us. Would things ever be the same again?[1]

Actually, Uncle Will, who was in his late twenties, not yet married, gay and debonair, was an amiable addition to the household. I recall one incident concerning him that is typical of the accidental, aleatory nature of the impressions a child's mind retains. Why one rather than another? Mystery.

I came into the down-stairs sitting-room, usually reserved for formal visits. In the middle of the room stood a couch—this was already anomalous—and on the couch, all I could see were layers of shaking blankets. "It's Uncle Will," someone explained, "Uncle Will has a chill." My delight in the rhyme stemmed further curiosity. "Uncle Will had a chill," and what it meant was no matter. I tiptoed out.

Another memory of Uncle Will is very clear. The date was 1898, and the United States was launching upon what was to be its first foreign imperialist adventure, the Spanish-American War (not however its first imperialist crime— ask the Navahos or the Iroquois, or the Cherokees . . .). Somehow I had picked up the words and tune of the popular song that was to be the "Tipperary" of that war. Uncle Will lifted me onto the table. "Come on, Maria, sing it for us. Sing 'Good-bye my Blue-Bell.'" Was I proud? And did I sing it *con gusto?* For you who surely never heard it, here it is in all its trite sadness:

> "Good-bye my Bluebell, Farewell to you.
> Just let me look into your eyes so blue.
> Mid campfires gleaming, mid shot and shell,
> I shall be dreaming of my own Bluebell."

Where have all the Bluebells gone? It is not entirely impossible that here and there across the country, may still be found today an occasional nonagenarian who could answer "present" to that roll-call. Most of them, however, after a life of undisturbed confidence in the "manifest destiny" of their country, must have entered into final peace at some time between the smashing victory of 1945 and the brumous non-victory of Pan-Mun-Jon, in 1953. May those whose soldier sweethearts were the first to fall in the odious cause of empire have found reunion in heaven!; 1784 men lost their lives during the hardly four months of actual fighting.

---

1. But I cannot treat lightly, confining her to my own worm's-eye impressions, the reality of Cornelia Peake McDonald, whose eventful, at times harsh and heroic life spanned eighty-seven critical years—1822 to 1909—of the nation's history.

"Remember the Maine!" How can we forget it?[2]

❖ ❖ ❖

Still set in the first cocoon another scene comes to mind. I was playing alone and intently in the back-yard sand-box. Viney appeared in the kitchen door and with unusual solemnity said that Mother had ordered me to come upstairs. What had I done now?

To my embarrassment—children don't like to see adults cry—I realized that Mother had been crying. An open telegram lay on her table. So it was not something I had done. I waited. "Your grandfather is dead. I must go to Roanoke for his funeral. You will do what you are told while I am gone." "Yes'm." My grandfather, who was that? Dead. What was that? This was my first contact with death as well as my first and only recollection of Colonel George Watson Carr, grandson of Dabney Carr, who married his friend Thomas Jefferson's sister, Martha. As I grew older I learned that Col. Carr had been a violent, tyrannical man, that he loved his dogs and horses better than he loved his children, that after their mother died, he married his children's governess, which had been considered a mésalliance. When a half-sister, Sally, was born, the three remaining children (a sister, Alice, died young) had divided their time between the homes of two maternal aunts, in Charlottesville and on a remote country estate called "The Barons." Maria, for whom I was named, and whose ring I still wear, married and died in childbirth. So as adults there had remained only Mother and Uncle Will. Of course there was the half-sister, "poor Sally." But she was considered to be something of a catastrophe and cruelty being frequent in those to whom life has been cruel, she was never really accepted as anything but a less-than-half-sister. When I recall the grudging hospitality shown those lonely Siamese twins, Aunt Sally and her poor little mother who, sadly enough, had a speech defect which made her the butt of uncharitable imitation on the part of us savages, I can only be

2. Commenting on the territorial aggrandizement that the war settlement gave the United States, and the often cruel treatment that the American military inflicted on the Filipinos, Mark Twain wrote: . . . Only when a republic's life is in danger should a man uphold his government when it is in the wrong. There is no other time.

"This republic's life is not in peril. The nation has sold its honor for a phrase: 'My country right or wrong.' It has swung itself loose from its safe anchorage and is drifting, its helm in pirate hands. . . . We cannot withdraw from this sordid raid because to grant peace to those little people upon their terms—independence—would dishonor us. You have flung away Adams' phrase. . . . He said, 'An inglorious peace is better than a dishonorable war.' You have planted a seed, and it will grow . . ." (Mark Twain, in Letters from the Earth, Harper and Row, New York. c. 1906)

ashamed that not one of us seems to have had the minimum natural empathy that would have attenuated this pattern of exclusion. The fact is, however, that "poor Sally" was so humorless, so neurotic, that her visits, which always heightened Mother's nervous tension, came to be dreaded by us all. The dénouement was to come much later. When she was well over 60 a telegram signed by a neighbor, brought the news that she had hung herself in the attic of the Maine cottage that had been her home for many years.

◆ ◆ ◆

Ours being a very large family "connection"—I once counted over fifty first-cousins—a constant game of visiting musical-chairs was in progress among us children to acquaint us with our kith and kin not only in Louisville but throughout the Kentucky-Virginia-Tennessee triangle. I was sent to visit Uncle Hunter McDonald's family at their summer cabin near Nashville, as well as Father's sister, Aunt Nell, in Henderson, Kentucky. Here there were six children. One of the six was rather seriously retarded. But he was treated with the same gaiety and affection as the others, and whatever may have been their original distress over his condition, there was no trace of it.

Another visit, and a very exciting one it was, was to Uncle Will and his beautiful—even though "Yankee"—bride, a luminous brunette whom I remember almost exclusively in a many-ruffled white muslin dress, her glossy black hair piled high on top of her head, and wearing a wide yellow sash that hung to her skirt-hem in back.

At his father's death, Uncle Will had decided to invest his inheritance in the noble pursuit of "gentleman farming," and had immediately acquired all the trappings to go with it: a "gentleman's" home and farm-lands in Virginia, a beautiful young wife, thorough-bred horses, dogs and cattle, the required number of black retainers to keep all this in style. Alas, the inheritance had not been inexhaustible and by the time several babies had been added to the other responsibilities, this dream farm had to be abandoned for more realistic surroundings. As long as it lasted, however, I remember that every Christmas we received from Uncle Will a barrel of "Albemarle pippins" and a Collie pup. The pup usually ran away—always a source of tears—and the delicious apples were rapidly eaten. Uncle Will himself is still tenderly remembered.

Returning to this visit, my mind's cinema sees the romantic young couple climbing into a smart two-seated "trap," to which was hitched a sleek bay, held by a brown stable-boy who, although a little older than I, was also my frequent companion, there being no other children about.

One day, tired of playing, we came to rest beside a narrow grass-bordered stream, hardly two feet wide and fed from a nearby spring. My initiation into

what for me was the mystery of structural difference, although it never went beyond the ludic context, has nevertheless by virtue, I suppose, of its explosive poten-
tial, three quarters of a century later, not been forgotten.

He sat on one bank, I on the other; the water between us was deep. We
looked across at each other and smiled. But soon my eyes were drawn irresistibly
from his face to something that he was showing me. What was it? A little chip-
munk, perhaps? But why did he keep it there in his trousers? I stared, fascinated;
the bright-eyed little creature seemed to be gazing back at me across the water,
its owner dreamily smiling. Since I had never seen one like it, I still remember it.

❖ ❖ ❖

Quite evidently, Mother's[3] had been a bleak postwar childhood. One of the aunts,
Aunt Letty, was married to an overbearing Frenchman, Dr. Francis Sorel. (The
adjective was Mother's). I was taken to visit this childless couple as a little girl. I
even kissed the old gentleman's cheek, reluctantly however, for it looked stub-
bly and his smile was less than warm.

Mother recalled that as a "young lady" she had had the temerity to invite one
of her callers at "The Barons" to stay for supper, on an evening when the main
dish was oysters, no doubt the giant variety to be found in nearby Chesapeake
Bay. Innocently enough, the young man, finding the oysters over-large, cut them
with his dinner knife. This gesture, for Dr. Sorel, was so inexcusable that after
the guest had left he ordered Mother never again to invite that "vulgarian" to
his house; in any case he probably considered the entire United States to be a
slough of vulgarity, but then what had brought him there?[4] Like Col. George
Watson Carr, this great uncle, my first Frenchman, soon faded from my consciousness, except for the fact that my eldest sister was named Letitia Sorel, and
as I grew older this name evoked France, where I was destined to spend the
greater part of my adult life.[5]

3. Born 1860 in Roanoke, Virginia, [she] married Donald McDonald of Winchester, Virginia in 1888. I surmise that she had loved someone else very deeply. But this secret she kept
to herself and no trace of it remained after her death in 1935. Her album of girlhood photographs contained a number of photographs of young men, all respectfully inscribed to
"Miss Betsy Carr."

4. According to a plan of the Watts family graveyard, Dr. Sorel outlived Letitia Watts by
sixteen years. May he never again have been subjected to the offensive spectacle of a Virginia
yokel cutting oysters.

5. After over two centuries in the new world, I was the first, in either my mother's or my
father's family to return to live in the world from which their ancestors had sprung. For my
Mother, this choice of mine was all but treasonable and she decided that, after her death,

Mother's other aunt, the former Alice Watts, who married twice, had a household that consisted of "my child, your children, our children and my sister's children," which left little for the last named, a situation they recalled with some bitterness. The widow of Judge William Robertson of Charlottesville, at the time I visited there Aunt Alice was still living in her large antebellum house which, for many years, had seen no repair and little domestic service. The house was also the home of three of the first batch of Mother's septuagenarian Robertson cousins, of whom there remained two old ladies: cousin Betty, almost blind, tiny, bent double and saintly, with a black mustache and a permanent crochet needle in her hand; and cousin Lucy, somewhat younger and slightly but harmlessly mad. Her eyes gleamed whenever the conversation assumed a gay or mundane character, when it turned perchance to Byron, or to "Mr. Addison and Mr. Steele." One day she asked me if I had noticed how many crazy people there were in Charlottesville. "I'm crazy too," she commented, "but I meet lots of others," was her frequent observation as she recounted her adventures during her daily streetcar rides. Mother pointed out to me a few doors away, on the same street, the house of a family who had solved the problem of their mad member in a most original manner. Like the other houses on that street this one was set far back from the carriage road surrounded by a vast lawn planted with tall old trees, which made it possible for their lunatic to be aired in a comfortable, screened cage, from where he could watch the passing scene at a safe distance. How friendly end humane! Nobody was "put away," the tie with home was not broken; this illness was like any other. It too needed love and security.

The third member of Aunt Alice's household, cousin Edward, I heard and sensed, but never saw. He was rumored to be ill with *locomotor ataxia* (a disease not to be mentioned before a young girl), so the sound of his shuffling steps in the hall, or occasional little cries of distress and pain, were the only signs of his presence that reached me except for the discreet comings and goings of a black man-servant designated for his care. "Poor Edward," as he was usually referred to, was probably one of many life-long victims—no penicillin—of the "wild oats" tradition that at one time was all but obligatory among self-respecting young bloods at the University of Virginia.

Another witness to those roaring years was the three-storey, long-closed, round brick structure that stood behind the big house—it was still touchingly referred to as "the boy's house"—and was by then entirely overgrown, even the door,

---

none of the so-called "family heirlooms" would come to me, since I lived "abroad." And how prescient was this decision! Through circumstances that I shall describe later, we actually did, during the Second World War, lose the greater part of all our possessions in Paris.

with tough, old ivy. According to legend, this had been the haven in which the wildest orgies could be slept off unmolested and unlectured, since none but concerned males were allowed access; particularly was what went on there *not* the affair of the ladies of the house who, I was told, had preferred it that way.

These oddities notwithstanding, on the surface, life in Aunt Alice's house reflected her own serene, dignified personality. At 7 o'clock she was downstairs, fully dressed, her soft white hair becomingly combed, usually at her desk, since this was the hour when she wrote to her many absent relatives: already, the day before, the addressed envelopes of the letters she planned to write the next morning lay in a neat pile, awaiting their contents. After breakfast, she put on a wide apron, and herself washed the preceding day's table silver in large pans of hot water brought to the dining room from the outdoor kitchen. The motives for this ritual were never actually formulated, but the imagination can find a certain number. On wintry days there was always a pleasant coal fire in the grate—sufficient in any case to warm the calves of your legs—, and in season, there were flowers or branches in the vases.

On one of these Charlottesville visits, I accompanied Mother on a pilgrimage to the former home of Thomas Jefferson, Monticello, a few miles above the town. After many years of neglect on the part of absent owners, the place had been bought by a New Yorker, a Mr. Levey, who was known to be in residence. This news had incited Mother, whose ancestor-worship was positively Confucian, to write for permission "to visit the graves of her great-grandparents, the former Martha Jefferson and her husband Dabney Carr," to whom Jefferson had extended eternal hospitality. Mother feared—and her fears were amply justified —that the near century during which Monticello had gone more or less untended would have left the small plot of informally hallowed ground (the graves were just beside the house as I remember) in a state of neglect.

There was great hilarity among the old cousins when Mr. Levey replied with a cordial invitation to lunch for us both. Imagine going to lunch with that vulgar Yankee—he could not be otherwise—and of all places, at Monticello! Cousin Betty, ever the gentle Christian, conceded that he might be a kind, good man, nevertheless. But crazy Lucy's eyes beamed with ironic intensity: "You'll eat on gold plates!" she prophesied, gloating. I have no recollection of gold plates, merely of an excellent lunch, presided by a pleasant, knowledgeable host, who afterwards allowed Mother to rake the earth and redress the sunken grave-stones to her heart's content, while I wandered through the garden. Stupidly enough, I did not listen to the decisions taken, so I have no idea as I write this whether Martha and Dabney are still there (I'm inclined to think that they are), or whether they have been removed to a more discreet hereafter. What they should have, it seems to me, is peace. But no doubt the status of "National Shrine," to which

Monticello has since been raised, hardly makes for that. And the thousands of tourists who, after visiting the University, contemplating Jefferson's beautiful rotunda and "snake-wall," while listening to the guide's lurid account of Edgar Allan Poe's brief and dissolute stay among those patinated bricks would, I guess, have little respect for the repose of two such minor figures as Martha and Dabney. But I'm anticipating.

In the early days of the new century people in the defeated South were still generally sad and poor, life was disorganized, often hard. Mother used to say that, as a child, she had thought that a long bleak crepe veil was the badge of a grown woman. And this in spite of the fact that neither Roanoke where she was born, nor Charlottesville, where she spent most of her youth, had seen any actual fighting. Indeed, I am not entirely sure that Col. Carr, who was a West-Pointer, took any active part in the Civil War, which had so tragically marked the lives of my father's family. But the McDonalds lived in Winchester, Virginia, which was in the path of the armies.

Col. Angus McDonald, my other grandfather, although well over military age in 1861 (he was born in 1799), insisted on taking an active command, was captured and died, shortly after his release from prison, of the ill treatment he had received, according to witnesses. However incredibly, he had firmly believed in the future of the Confederacy: "With our slaves," he told his wife, "we'll become the most prosperous country in the world: both England and France are on our side. People will have cotton." According to Grandmother's diary, he was buried with full military honours (Confederate, of course), his coffin wrapped "in the folds of the stars and bars," as the old lady sentimentally described the scene. That the Federal command, having captured this doughty old rebel, should have felt no compunction about imprisoning him, appears only too logical, even though he was over 60 at the time!

I should perhaps apologize for this backward digression from the Spanish-American to the Civil War. When I was a child the South was not yet entirely on its feet; each year the "Confederate Reunion" brought together a less numerous group of garrulous, one-armed, one-legged old veterans; people with money were necessarily of "carpet-bagger," "yankee" origin; black-garbed ladies of "gentle" birth were still filling their over-large, run-down houses with boarders, while their daughters were emptying the chamber-pots. Here, of course, I am speaking principally of Virginia; Kentucky had been a divided state and neither the disaster nor the sense of defeat and resentment were comparable. But my parents had not moved to Kentucky until after their marriage. Like Jefferson, who, when questioned as to the original home of his family, replied that he had "never heard them speak of any place but Virginia," they too felt and talked as Virginians. And for men and women with this background, even as late as 1914, the word "war" inevitably gave back echoes of 1861–1865, with its aftermath of loss and decay.

◆ ◆ ◆

Chapter II

Just when the move took place I am not quite sure. One thing I do remember, however, is that the new century which was ushered in with much rhetorical fanfare[6] found us living in St. James Court, a greener, more spacious cocoon in which, unlike the tight corner at "Brook and Oak," a child could be given wide range and complete liberty, the occasional horse-drawn vehicles constituting no threat. Hop-scotch, catchers, statues, hi-spy, farmer-in-the-well, Miss-Jenny-Anne-Jones, cop-'n-robbers, not forgetting tree-climbing, rafter-walking, winter-sledding, a four-passenger goat-wagon and a wee Shetland pony. . . . for years filled the nearly four hours of afternoon freedom that the 8:30 to 1:30 school day made possible.

In 1900 there were still many building sites for sale in St. James Court—about 15, I should think—and games on the vacant lots, plus the thrill of playing in houses still under construction (I was a sure-footed rafter-walker) lent pioneer zest to life in the new neighbourhood.

"The Court" stretched North-South from Magnolia Street to Hill Street, both of which led to zones of different but equally intense enjoyment. Just beyond Hill Street, which was always sweetly redolent of a nearby tobacco factory, there was a livery-stable whose friendly boss allowed us to visit the horses in their stalls; while at the other end, Magnolia Street bordered on a small public park with giant trees, and slopes for sledding, that had recently been presented to the city by the owners, a branch of the Wilmington Dupont family, some of whom still lived in the park.

The former Meta Dupont, who was now a widow with three children: Greta, about my age, Alfred and Arthur Coleman, made her home with her sister, Miss Zara Dupont, "Miss Sadie" to us. Both women seemed to live entirely for the three fatherless children and their house was a place we loved to go to. I recall the weekly dancing classes with Miss Sadie at the piano, accompanying us in the Lancers—tatatatah, ta-tah, ta-tah (remember?)—the Virginia reel and many of the square dances that are again so popular in the United States. The lemonade that followed was particularly appreciated.

The Coleman family later moved into the Court and the old house was razed. Here as before, the children had a large playground and even a long, low

6. It was to be the "century of the child" prophesied by the, at that time, well-known Scandinavian writer, Ellen Key.

playhouse, both of which were enjoyed by all the neighbourhood children who gathered there to play ball, croquet, tennis and an endless game we called "horse-show." This involved imitation by two-legged humans of the paces performed for exhibition by four-legged animals, an accomplishment for which some of us were more talented than others. Blue, red, white and yellow ribbons were seriously awarded by a jury of experts and we neighed and stamped our feet realistically while awaiting their decisions.

As I recall, my own talents in this line were limited to the canter and trot, while Greta Coleman was herself so convinced that she was a horse, that she was able to add to these basic paces the much more intricate "rack," which is a combined trot and canter, with "all four feet being off ground together at once," to quote my eminently serious Oxford dictionary. I regret that I have no photograph of Greta performing this act of levitation but I recall that she won most of the blue ribbons with it.

A great adventure was the purchase with our own pocket-money of a rickety old horse marked for the stockyards, whom we baptised "Charity" and vowed to restore to health and happiness. The brushing and currying of Charity's poor, mangy coat, care of his stall, water-bucket and feed-bag, proved to be the source of never-ending activity and interest. These were also the kinds of responsibility that very soon only appealed to a few true believers, which eliminated rough older boys, such as Donald [Jolas's older brother] and his gang of cynical robber-barons, and allowed us to pursue our dream of total rehabilitation for Charity, untaunted and in peace.

After a few weeks, although nothing could hide those protruding ribs, to our indulgent eyes, Charity seemed to be as ready as he ever would be for a test of the results of our pedagogical methods: we would hitch him to the "trap" and judge, in action, his improvement; a very ambitious project that required both manpower and method.

For the trap had long been in disuse as also the harness, which required mending, cleaning, rubbing and polishing, in addition to preparing Charity himself for the event.

As I reconstruct the Charity episode, I have the impression that we worked not only days but weeks—months?—to prepare for this apotheosis. And above all I see myself as having been of little faith. Indeed, but for Greta, who dismissed with contempt all doubts and objections, I fear that the project might have fallen through. But Greta was not only the eldest, she was also a Dupont; she it was who had had the vision, it would, it must, succeed.

And what's more, it did succeed. That is, after having been sponged, curried and brushed beyond all recognition, Charity was actually hitched to a by now immaculately clean trap, his harness rubbed and shining. He made the trip along the back alley-way from Hill Street to Magnolia, lifting his poor tired feet valiantly as he had been so painstakingly taught to do during weeks of intensive training.

Voice: What happened then, Granny?

Just here, time draws a curtain. But I suspect that the older generation, even two such saints as the Dupont sisters, decided that enough was enough, and that they succeeded in smuggling the poor creature out of the stable under cover of night. This last bit, however, is my invention. But the rest is not. In addition to its pedagogical value, rehabilitating Charity was also an excellent introduction to the virtues of organized labour and a firm command that itself is fired by faith.

◆ ◆ ◆

School for me, was an exhilarating adventure. I started in the public school that, because of its location, we called "Second and Hill." It was a recent, well-planned building with drinking fountains and a big playground, where learning held no terrors for anybody. Already, on the way there, the deliciously penetrating odor from the neighbouring tobacco factory left an enduring reminder of those first autumn mornings on my olfactive nerves that I have only to recall to evoke an entire canvass of people and places.

But these first school days are also the background against which I set some of my earliest and happiest musical impressions. On rainy days, "with shoulders back and heads erect," "marching on, marching on in sin-gle file," we "stepped care-ful-ly through every aisle," to the march from Bellini's <u>Norma.</u> I remember that we also sang Mendelssohn's <u>Over hill, over dale</u>, which had a lilt that delighted us all.[7] And when we reached the lines: "And I serve the fairy queen, To dew her orb upon the green," sung in solo by one William Hollingsworth (all of 7 years old, I imagine) whose clear boy-soprano left me blissful with admiration . . . just to recall that moment, is to feel grateful to the gay little teacher with the good Czech name of Swoboda, who planted that seed in our child ears. Where are you now, William Hollingsworth? Has your own voice, soaring high above the class-room, beyond the sweet-potato vines in the tall windows, haunted you as it has me? Or are you not there to reply, already under the beautifully green sod of that fairest of cemeteries, Cave Hill? You are not forgotten.

◆ ◆ ◆

After a year in a rented house, at No 32 St. James Court, we moved to No 40, which Father bought, and which with a certain number of periodic alterations: an upstairs back wing, as little children grew into big ones, an extended front

---

7. Neither Shakespeare, Mendelssohn nor "A Midsummer Night's Dream" were mentioned, but we were bound to find out these noble origins one day.

porch for summer night singing and conviviality, a small room off the dining room for intimate talk, a large living-room made from two smaller ones, for a piano and dancing, a bathroom here, another there—all excitedly experienced as improvements, and all designed by Father himself who, although an engineer, had once worked for the architectural firm of his older brothers—this was to remain our family home until Mother's death, in 1935.

According to legend, St. James Court owed its harmonious proportions of two oval tree-bordered lawns separated by a fountain, and its aristocratic name —further Londonized to include two smaller side courts, Fountain and Belgravia —to the fact that it had originally been the site of an Exposition held there before our time. We knew about Expositions. In 1904 there was one in St. Louis (full title, "Louisiana Purchase Exposition"), from which our parents and their friends brought back exotic "souvenirs" and gay anecdotes. The Louisville event, we concluded, had probably been of the same order and we were content to leave it in its hazy limbo.

As time passed however, and Louisville ceased to be the geographical center of our universe, we occasionally asked ourselves: Why Louisville? Why should this relatively obscure little city on the southern bank of the Ohio have been chosen for an event that, with its inauguration by the President of the United States, was to be given a national prominence out of all proportion to its more than likely lazy, provincial rhythm? Today, in line with the recent mood of "retro" interests, a few enterprising Louisvillians, mostly latter-day residents of "the Court," have brought to light information that does, to some extent, answer the question: Why Louisville? And this choice, far from having been a hat-pin hazard, would appear to have been dictated by a complex of economic and political considerations that furnish pertinent explanations of the curiously "split" city I grew up in. Here I shall open a backward-looking parenthesis.

In 1880, 15 years had passed since the end of the shattering events of 1861– 1865. The turbulent reconstruction era had brought little peace, the opposite of prosperity, and much bitterness. In Washington, reference to the southern states as "conquered provinces" to be "disposed of at will by the conquerors," had not helped matters: and economically, the condition of most of the South had been desperate.[8] In addition, "carpet bagger"[9] politicians were travelling through the

8. A reminder: "Means of transport were destroyed; railways and bridges were ruined; Southern securities were valueless, the Confederate currency system was completely disorganized. Emancipated negroes wandered idly from place to place . . ." Article entitled "United States" in the Encyclopedia Britannica of 1941.

9. "Term of contempt originally for wildcat bankers who defrauded the people of a community and decamped, but eventually for Northern men who went to the South after the

region in an attempt to organize a black vote in favor of the Republican Party, a move that met with resentment on the part of the defeated Confederates.[10]

(Lest we forget.) As late as 1872, in order to separate rival factions, the capitals of Louisiana, Arkansas and Alabama were occupied by Federal troops, and a few State governments had become so corrupt that only New York City and certain branches of the Federal government offered parallel scandals. The spoils system—"to the victor belong the spoils"—was generally practised and it was during this same epoch that the Secretary of War was obliged to resign to avoid impeachment for corruption in the conduct of Indian Affairs. As one commentator wrote with admirable understatement: "It was a time of lax post-war public morals."

But that was not all. There was also the fact, as we have witnessed in our own century, that speculation and the rapid growth of great fortunes usually accompany wars. The Civil War was no exception. It too had furnished the occasion for acquiring sudden wealth, and this wealth was looking for new investment possibilities. Where, more logically, would these possibilities lie than in the still prostrate South?

When President Garfield was assassinated in September 1881, his Vice-President, Chester Arthur, well-known "spoils-man" and former Director of Customs for the Port of New York (from which post he had been removed for alleged corruption by President Hayes) stepped into the Presidential shoes. It was by Chester Arthur, then, that the "Southern Exposition" was inaugurated in 1883 in Louisville, Kentucky, which, we recall, was a border state and had remained technically neutral[11] during the war. What more ideal place for such an exposition? Indeed, where else at that time, could it have been so strategically located? I imagine that it was not entirely for motives of municipal patriotism that Louisville came to be dubbed the "Gateway of the South."

There follows the question: Who composed the group of enterprising Louisville businessmen that planned and carried out the "Southern Exposition"? Could they not have included some of the "carpet-baggers" who were to be so resented

---

Civil War to live, especially to seek private gain under the often corrupt reconstruction governments." (Merriam-Webster Dictionary, Springfield, Mass. 1940).

10. The following choice morsel turned up in the US press in mid-April, 1975. "The United States Senate has voted to restore full citizenship to General Robert E. Lee . . . Lee was denied amnesty because a signed oath of allegiance to the United States . . . was lost and never reached President Johnson . . . It was since discovered in the National Archives." Lee died in 1870.

11. I take the occasion slightly to modify this statement since, in 1864, when Gen. Sherman was moving on Atlanta, Louisville served as his supply base.

by indigenous Southerners? Probably. And in addition to the legacy of St. James Court—for which I thank them, it was a happy place—what else did this Exposition do for the city? The answer may well be that it kept it from slipping gently into the Ohio river, out of sheer inanition. So much for commerce and "progress."

Socially, however, I am inclined to think that it may have widened and exacerbated the gulf that already existed between the business community and the landed or professional "gentry," a pattern of separation that had been handed down with the Anglo-Virginia tradition. In any case, the Louisville of my youth was socially still highly stratified. Is it today? I wouldn't know. But I do not hesitate to say that when I was growing up, the most arbitrary, palpable social lines were drawn, in addition to which racial taboos were implacable. My mother's pigeonholes were, in fact, so numerous and so shocking that I can't refrain from enumerating them here, if only for the incredulity that they inevitably arouse today. They were, in diminishing order: "high-born ladies and gentlemen" (actual or former land-owners,[12] distinguished professionals: churchmen, military, judges, teachers, lawyers, doctors . . . no dentists or veterinarians, however!); "tacky" well-born ladies and gentlemen, i. e., those who failed to observe the standards of their ancestors; educated, nice, decent, or vulgar "common" people; the shop-keeper class; the "overseer" class (a throwback to Virginia); the working class; poor white trash.

There also lived in Louisville several highly educated, talented Jewish families who, I imagine, were uninterested in the round of frivolities—the elaborate dinners, ladies' luncheons and afternoon card-parties, the débutante balls and Derby breakfasts—that filled the lives of this stranded tribe of English "cavaliers." But Mother's categories did not include them, she may even have been intimidated by them, her own formal educational advantages having been so few. Also, they kept to themselves except when it was a question of improving Louisville's civic or cultural status, for which much is owed them. Exceptionally, an occasional "distinguished Jewish gentleman," or foreigner, who enjoyed a game of bridge and possessed the social amenities, participated in the tribal rites. But they were few, which fact enhanced the charm of their exoticism.

Actually, who were the foreigners in Louisville? I remember a vinegary, very handsome old French gentleman, indignant with his own country for having dethroned the Virgin Mary in favor of the "Goddess of Reason"; a mysterious,

---

12. "Stock rearing, experience and knowledge of what kinds are profitable and where and how . . . ; a knowledge of tillage, fields to be sown with crops and fields planted for fruit; of bee-keeping and of rearing such birds and fishes as can contribute. Those are the three main branches of the most proper way of making a living." Aristotle: The Politics, Book 1, 11.

highly successful German industrialist, who dealt in metals, but having founded a numerous common-law family, he was only known to husbands.[13] In addition to a handful of German and Italian grocers and bakers,[14] there were plenty of Irish who owned the best-run, gayest pubs in town, from whose exclusively masculine fastnesses came the best jokes and the tallest tales about all the unpublished goings-on both inside and outside the "pale," especially in the very colorful, swarming political life of the city. But they were hardly to be counted as foreigners. Together with a handful of frequently Jewish intellectuals from other cities, who came to work in the editorial offices of the local newspapers, these bright Irishmen formed a nucleus of intelligence and wit that we younger members of the closed-in "gentry" longed to know better.

And the blacks? What of those native-born foreigners, "equal though separate," loved though removed, not yet feared? For Mother, they too fell naturally into well-defined categories: self-respecting, well-behaved colored people, among whom house-servants were recruited: they "knew their place" and said "Yes ma'am" and "No ma'am" (for that matter, so did we children); unobjectionable, lazy "darkies"; "uppity" insolent Negroes who talked back and were therefore unemployable, as were, also, the so-called "cornfield" blacks, who could only be employed out-of-doors.

In view of all that has happened since, I realize that I shall need a diplomat's tact and little George Washington's moral fearlessness if I am to avoid some unpleasant accusations. It should be remembered, however, that I speak from inside a situation into which I was born; that understanding of its iniquities—so suavely concealed that the preposterous fiction upon which the entire structure reposed, seemed to be "a law of nature"—could only come with growing up. I realize today that I accepted too docilely and for too long, the hypocritical premises that justified the system. They were nowhere questioned however, neither at home, at school, at Church nor in the local press. And particularly, one sensed no hostility on the part of the blacks themselves, which made for lazy acquiescence to the *status quo*. Since I am writing this in September 1975, I ask myself if, instead of living for over 50 years in France, where there is no legal segregation, I had spent those years in Louisville, would I or would I not today be lying

---

13. *Anthropological note:* It was an accepted social tenet that a woman of "good breeding," by virtue of this fact, could more easily raise the social status of her husband of lesser origin than a man placed in an analogous position. In other words, the transmission of hereditary factors was believed to be matrilineal.

14. The popcorn or icecream man was inevitably Italian, and failing a "well-trained colored girl," it was the dream of Louisville house-keepers to find that rare pearl, a "clean, hard-working German girl" to serve as chambermaid.

face downward with the anti-busing demonstrators? Here I am reminded of Anthony Eden's almost apologetic reply to the interviewer who in the film "Le chagrin et la pitié" asked if Britons would have collaborated: "I really cannot say, we were never occupied." Nor were my children ever faced with being forcibly transported to a distant, inferior type school to redress the wrongs of the society in which they lived.

I have followed from a distance the civil-rights action with warm sympathy for all the hard-won gains and the terrible cost to the black community in America. I have made friends among American blacks in Paris. But I know that this is not enough. And to what extent early reflexes have conditioned and limited my empathy which, although genuine has not been militant, I cannot say. As for busing, I would undoubtedly be opposed to it, though not for the same reasons, probably, as the prone demonstrators.

In my opinion it is not a solution. This purely behaviorist prescription for curing the combination of fear, despising and envy that composes race prejudice reminds me of the remedy once recommended by certain simplistic educators for curing characterical instability by means of disciplined hand-writing practice; the current adjective would be "cosmetic."

For the evil is the result of centuries of conditioning. Rooted in the timeless master-slave context, it took refuge after 1865 in mindless, defiant "Jim Crow" laws that refused to envisage any situation other than that of total segregation: neighborhoods, schools, offices, churches, shops, theatres, cafés, restaurants, public transport, public parks, public libraries, and hospital services were all segregated in Louisville when I was growing up. It is not altogether surprising therefore that today still, neighborhoods and schools should be the objects of die-hard resistance. Let it be whispered in a middle-class white neighborhood that a black family has bought the house on the corner, a rush to sell before prices drop is a familiar phenomenon that real-estate dealers in many cities know only too well how to exploit. The white families will move, usually to the suburbs, leaving behind a new—segregated—black neighborhood, while creating elsewhere a new —segregated—white one. The vicious circle of separation lives on, a serpent biting its tail. And once again, no normal contacts can exist otherwise than through some such exhausting, artificial procedure as busing. This is the situation that exists in Louisville and elsewhere across the country as I write today.

Not content with having penalized the black children by giving them inferior schools, the national law-makers who dreamed up this aberrant plan decided to penalize the white children as well by forcing them to attend these same inferior schools. What nonsense! All schools should be desegregated, all teachers should be equally well-trained and well-paid; adequate new schools should be built wherever needed and *temporary* voluntary busing, *for black children only,* should be organized to let them benefit by the, at present, better white schools. The day when even this busing is abandoned because it is no longer needed will mean that the American people have finally abandoned their Ku-Klux ways and thought this problem through to its only decent conclusion.

> If parents, black and white, got together and forced the Boston school system to provide equal education, you could keep your children in your neighborhood and I could keep my children in mine. Instead, my children get up at 5:30 a.m. They leave at 6:30 a.m. to catch a bus out to the suburbs. They arrive home after 4 p.m. My five-year-old spends 2¼ hours in school and two hours in transportation every day.
>
> All I can say is that your fight has just begun. The black race has been fighting for 400 years to prove we're human beings, with the same wants and needs of everyone else.
>
> Joyce Sinclair
> Boston

Letter to:
Time, Oct. 6, 1975

Neighborhood segregation is probably a relic of life on the plantation, where the slave quarters were at a distance from the big house. But today it is primarily, as well, a consequence of the black workers' usually inferior salary. The older black neighborhoods were already far from the white center and I, for one, do not remember as a child meeting in St. James Court any blacks except those who worked in our home or in the homes of our neighbors.

Just here it is interesting to recall the relationship that obtained between these domestic workers and the white families, both adults and children, that composed the households. But I shall say in advance that my description will be limited to the household I knew best, which was my own.

A feature of southern family life, still in my time, was the elderly black "mammy." If the children were numerous, she usually remained part of the household, in which she occupied a special place, until her death. Or, if the children were few, she divided her time between two or three families[15] leading more or less

---

15. The case of a "mammy" who nursed one of my nephews, in 1918, has remained indelibly in my memory. A tall, handsome, unusually light-skinned woman in her late sixties, she was greatly beloved by all who knew her. One day she was officially informed that she was not the child of the black family in which she had grown up, but had been a foundling deposited on their doorstep, and was of white origin. No one who has never lived in a racist society can measure the emotion that this news aroused, especially among whites. Would this hitherto "black" woman seize this opportunity to "pass over," to escape from her accidentally

parallel lives, in the same way that a seamstress, a "party-waiter" or a "yard-man" did. Mammy was the pillar, the ancestral figure, whose total devotion and constant presence greased the wheels of adaptation to the arrival of the new baby. She it was who rocked and sang it to sleep, who brought it to the mother for nursing, who bathed and dressed it, patted and soothed its colics, passed the often sleepless nights that today most young parents pass unaided. The man or woman who has had the infant privilege of falling asleep on the shoulder of one of these kind old women, dreamily rocking and crooning, the baby held close, cheek to cheek, knows, from having experienced it, how surely human tenderness can communicate hearts-ease and comfort.

When I was getting to be a "big girl," ten or eleven years old, and we no longer had a baby of our own at home, I remember rising very early to join a little gathering of neighborhood mammies who, in particularly hot weather, preferred to air their charges in the "cool of the morning," and let them sleep later in a darkened room made tolerable by the slight cross-current of air furnished by bowed shutters. From time to time they would allow me to hold a baby in my arms, which gave me an immense sense of pride and fulfillment. "What are little girls made of?" goes the song. Certainly not only of "sugar and spice and everything nice."

❖ ❖ ❖

In silent agreement that the fundamental assumptions would not be questioned —and they were not—there was, miraculously, an atmosphere of mutual respect and courtesy; let's not exaggerate: of respectful black execution of courteously given white orders. There was also, of course, the traditional white paternalism that assumed responsibility in times of illness or trouble (usually with the police or bill-collector). Finally, there was no hostility that I remember. There was even frequently genuine friendliness, lots of talk, joking and singing. No liberties, however, on either side; above all no "impertinence," black servants "knew their place."[16]

Conversely the slightest disrespect shown a black servant by a white child, such as use of the word "nigger," which was forbidden under all circumstances,

---

acquired negritude? She did not take long to make her decision: she had been black all her life, the people she loved were black, she would remain one.

16. An incident that occurred in a "gentleman's club" is revealing of the time. A club member who had been drinking rather heavily struck a black waiter. He was blackballed from the club by a majority vote of the members for having struck a man "who could not strike back."

was soundly punished. Nor was he or she allowed to give an order.[17] Later, when these same white children who had lived in close intimacy with the blacks since birth, reached early adolescence, they were ordered to keep their distance, drop "undue" familiarity, and not forget that they should be addressed as "Miss" and "Mister" preceding their first name, by these, their oldest friends. At first, this passage was awkward, even cruel, but such were the rules of the game, and after a few months, the new relationship gradually became accepted as being the natural consequence of growing up within the context of the tribal law. Another generation of the superior race was preparing to assume "the white man's burden." For me, as a girl, I sensed disturbing, unspoken implications in this mutation, and one incident—a resounding slap given me because I had walked through the hall in my petticoat (which left arms and chest bare)—was justified by the fact that a *black man* working there had seen me. I must have been all of twelve years old. The law was unwritten, but like fear at sea, or in the air, punishment lay just beneath the surface; when a black man touched a white woman, the answer was lynching.

Here, an incident that occurred when my father was a very young man, is still a source of solace when I think of the tenacity of prejudice in my country. The date was probably 1885, or thereabouts, my father was working as a scout for the architectural firm of his older brothers, and his duties required him to visit many small Kentucky towns known to be planning new public buildings.

On one of these visits, he was surprised to find the town all but emptied of its inhabitants, except for a few infirm old men chatting on the public square. "Where is everybody?" Father asked. "Gone to the lynching," was the reply. They pointed toward a road leading out of town. "You can't miss it, just keep walking."

When Father arrived at the spot, what he saw was a determined, loud-mouthed white bully haranguing a crowd, and beside him, a terrified, cowed black. "All in favor of hanging say yes," shouted the master-of-ceremonies, and the crowd agreed in unison. Then, just as a formality, he added: "Anybody opposed?" Father stepped forward: "I am opposed." "And who the hell are you?" came the quick, angry retort. Father identified himself. "And I don't intend to stand here and see a man hung without fair trial." He was 6 ft. 4 inches tall, young and strong as an ox. But above all he was convinced and convincing, and in the end, the crowd agreed that the man should be returned to the jail and given "fair trial." Today, 90 years later, we have a Federal anti-lynch law. But the fact is that between 1882

---

17. No "personal service" was to be expected; servants' work did not include "picking up" after anybody, either child or adult.

and 1946 there were 4,715 lynchings in the United States, ¾ of them were blacks and %₀ of them took place in the South.[18]

❖ ❖ ❖

"Separate but Equal"

According to my Mother's housekeeping code, the food served in the kitchen although plentiful and of good quality, was not the same as that served in the dining-room—"they don't like the things we like." Nor was the table service the same. In fact, everything in daily use—china, glass, cutlery, all household linen, beds (particularly beds and blankets), once they had served for the blacks were limited to their use, and the rare white chamber-maid was not expected to sleep on a bed that had been used by blacks.

I remember describing this odious state of affairs to the Senegalese writer-diplomat, Alioune Diop, who was leaving Paris for a meeting of the United Nations. I still see his beautiful, long fingers, their joined tips forming a gothic arch, as he listened. "A Christian nation!" was his only comment.

❖ ❖ ❖

But these random socio-demographic notes cannot be closed without some reference to the only really indigenous inhabitants of Kentucky, those whose presence there has been pushed so far back into our memory store that it has seemed quite natural for me to leave them till the end, when I should have begun with them . . . the Indians.

The fact is however that although the wooden Indian, complete with toma-hawk and feathered head-dress, was still posted at the door of every Louisville tobacco-shop, I do not recall having seen any live Indians in Kentucky. I saw a good many during the several summer vacations that we spent in the back-waters of Lake Michigan, at Wequetonsing, or on Black Lake, not far from Petoskey. I have in fact an indelible memory of having discovered, as a little girl, probably five or six years old, the body of a drowned Indian, floating in a shady, sluggish stream that ran through the grounds of the hotel in which we were stopping. I gave the alert, and within minutes was surrounded by weeping squaws and tragic-faced men. The branches of the trees that bordered the stream hung low over the floating, fully dressed body; blood flowed from one ear. But at this point my recollections go blank; I had probably been hurried away by whatever hand had been supposed to have me in tow.

---

18. <u>The Negro in America</u>, by Arnold Rose, p. 186. Beacon Press, Boston, 1944.

We learned very young that our state had been the "dark and bloody ground" (or *Kentucke*) of fratricidal struggles between the Iroquois and the Cherokees; very ancient, giant trees in Louisville's two beautiful parks, Cherokee and Iroquois, where we loved to go for picnics, still bore traces of Indian inscriptions; the musical Indian names of our bordering rivers: the Ohio, the Mississippi, the Tennessee—all recalled those first inhabitants. There was also "Indian summer," that tenderest of seasons . . . but however current the expression, now used throughout the land, why this supplement of soft autumn days was given this name, would appear to be forgotten.

When I was young, more than a century had passed since the Indians had been driven further westward, after, bitter fighting, by our ancestors, whose chief claim to be remembered by their descendents was the role they had played in the euphemistically called "Indian Wars." Today's population must be hardly aware of anything more than the legend, although if they laid their ears to the ground they might well hear echoes of the twentieth-century war-cry of the AIM (American Indian Movement) and its demands that justice finally be done them.

In recent years, in Paris, I have met and worked with militants of AIM. There is a noble tenacity in their arguments that one cannot but admire. One would wish, for their sakes, that their goals were more realistic, however just their cause.

◆ ◆ ◆

If I have tended to dwell on these aspects of my youth, it is perhaps because these are the features about which, in Europe particularly, I have been most frequently questioned, not to say goaded. And each time I have attempted to describe them as they were,[19] I have been aware of barely concealed skepticism on the part of my listeners. "Really? The atmosphere was warm and friendly? There was no hostility?" And although the more polite among them may seem to accept my version, I am conscious of an unspoken accusation.

My own explanation of a short-lived reconciliation is to be found in the events that marked the post-war reconstruction years. With Lincoln dead, the vindictiveness with which certain Northern politicians had sought to punish the Confederates brought tragic harm to both whites and blacks. It is therefore not impossible, or so it seems to me, that as the war-time children of both races grew to adulthood, when they met again, with all the horror and suffering behind them, and in a new perspective of peace and security, they were in reality ready

---

19. Here of course I am speaking of black-white relations.

to resume an association that had not been only oppressive, whatever its basic iniquities.

But I shall leave to more learned researchers—historians, sociologists and the other social scientists—to analyse this brief moment of feudal harmony. All I have wanted to do was to bear witness to the fact that in one household that I knew well—my own—it did obtain, in all its fragile ambiguity, as an apparently happy "way of life" (some were no doubt happier than others), as late as World War I.

◆ ◆ ◆

I once said to my friend Richard Wright that I had not known any white families like the ones he described in "Black Boy." His reply: "I never knew any other kind," may perhaps be explained by the fact that he was fifteen years younger than I, and the brief moment I experienced had no doubt vanished before the iron had entered into his soul. There was also the fact that mine had been a narrowly sheltered youth.

But to reply to Diop; we are not, and I fear never have been a truly Christian nation. Genocide, slavery, lynching, Jim Crow . . . were never sanctioned in the Sermon on the Mount. But where are the Christian nations today? Has the ideal been too difficult of attainment? So difficult, that only large doses of hypocrisy have made it possible to pursue it thus far?

The late Irish poet, Padraic Colum, once asked me: "If you thought about it, could you imagine a better religion than Christianity?" Probably not, and if that gentle, good man himself were to be taken as model, certainly not. But if we look at what is happening on his own little island, we see that the interminable Ulster war is a war between rich and poor Christians, and even with no element of race or color to exacerbate it, the old demons of intolerance and will-to-dominate have turned these lamentable Christians into assassins: no justice, no love, above all, no Christianity.

But this is only one of the manifestations of decline. Few Christian nations have resisted the temptation to torture and kill, humiliate and exploit. Can the original Christian ideal of brotherhood and charity still constitute a rampart against the violence and injustice that obtain today? I am skeptical. Nor do the other world religions and ideologies seem to offer greater hope.

The humanity of our time would appear to be perilously suspended between total neglect, total regimentation and total destruction.

And yet we have other options.

Sadly for me, because I was very happy at "Second and Hill," my mother decided that, left to myself, I would not be able to distinguish between "nice" and "common" friends. So she removed me to a small private school for girls only, the "Semple Collegiate School," named for Louisville's most distinguished woman intellectual, the geographer, Ellen Churchill Semple, who was rumored to have been the recipient of honors from important European universities.[20]

My father, proud though he was of his mother's rather touching cultural achievements—according to legend, she was "rarely without a book in her hand," and had taught china painting—was nevertheless firmly opposed to what he called "short-haired women and long-haired men," which was the generally accepted attitude of male Louisvillians. One father of two girls went so far as to declare that all he asked of his daughters was that they should "look pretty, smell sweet and talk stylish," all of which they did to perfection.

The *SCS*, as we called the school, does not seem to have left any scars on my psyche, other than those of omission, which is probably about all one could ask of what, in the preceding century, would have been called a "dame school." The teachers were generally pleasant women and, I imagine, adequately educated, although I remember with bleeding sensibility the howls of derision with which my elders, Letty and Donald, who felt superior in their "high-school" world, greeted my attempts to interpret one teacher's description of Shakespeare's place in English literature. "He was like the chandelier," I explained to the assembled dinner-table, (the teacher actually had used this illustration to make her point), and it was only through Father's firm intervention "I listened to you both," he said, "now I'm going to listen to Maria," that my tears of humiliation and fury were stanched. "A real chandelier" remained for some years a bantering family joke—how withering these jokes can be![21] describe persons of genuine or, more often, imagined, achievement.

<hr>

20. Ellen Churchill Semple ("Miss Patty" to Louisvillians). Although these rumors were true I have since read that she was actively contested by many of her fellow geographers for her tendency to fit widely divergent societies.

21. Sibling relationships, with their mysteriously determined affinities and antagonisms, can offer as great a diversity of probabilities as bridge hands. But although serious attempts have been made by psychologists and educators to attenuate this determinism, it usually remains intractable to any type of manipulation. In our household, where the arithmetic was: 2 plus 1 plus 2, or: girl-boy / girl / girl-boy, the middle digit, myself, very early opted to be a "cat that walks alone." When Letty was 13, Donald 11, I 9, Cornelia 6 and Angus 3, the pattern was already visible, and the only voice that could make itself heard over the frequently discordant din was Mother's firm, "You children stop quarreling!"

Not that it was always like that; there could be considerable group conviviality. But except for the two younger children, I recall little intimacy between individuals, and as adults, the divisions remained, deep, subterranean streams. But I shall not return to these imperfections in a family greatcoat that did, in fact, keep all of us warm for many years.

Actually, my memories of the *SCS* have little to do with the acquisition of knowledge: a gymnastics teacher who wore long, full black bloomers and a sailor blouse, taught us to walk on the balls of our feet; a sweet old "Miss Annie," who appeared at recess time with a clothes-basket from which she dispensed dough-nuts and milk; a witty little French woman from whom I learned *je suis, tu es, il est,* the mysteries of *la lune* and *le soleil,* as well as a ditty about *"la violette double, double . . ."* every word of which, learned parrot-like, I still remember. There was also, and for this I have always been grateful, a brief incursion into Latin—we even peeked into <u>De Bello Gallico</u>—and when on my arrival in France, my French teacher realized that I actually knew the difference between a dative and an accusative, she was incredulous. An American!

What else? Not much, really; little geography, precious little history except that concerned with Daniel Boone and his wily ways with the Indians. In the long run, too, I fear that I was not particularly drawn to the "nice" girls (which had been the reason for putting me in that school). In any case, when after gradu-ation, a modest University scholarship was proposed, this seemed such an improb-able solution to the problem of what to do with me next—I was 16—that it was quickly dismissed. By that time, my dominant interest was music—piano and lots of amateur singing—and it was generally agreed that I was more gifted for musi-cal than intellectual pursuits.

So the die was cast: music, yes, higher education, no. The *SCS* sheepskin, awarded at 16, would suffice to take me through life, and I would probably learn more as the years passed. But the fact is that I didn't know then what I didn't know. It has taken a long time and lots of living to learn even this. As for the rest, I'm here to look . . .

However inadequate my formal schooling, I learned some things from my parents: the difference between "mine and thine," and the converse, the subtle amenities of hospitality and such abstract notions as honor, tolerance, generos-ity, fragments that they had "shored against their ruin" over-shadowed years of their youth. . . .

◆ ◆ ◆

In addition to home and school, there was a third cocoon to which I became deeply attached: Sunday-School, then gradual, full-fledged church membership which, particularly in early adolescence, because it was so different from the other influences to which I was exposed, and set vibrating new chords of emotion and reflexion, became the source of initiation into beneficent, if only half-understood mysteries.

The catechism alone: "What is your name?" and the reply: "N or M," seemed to favor me particularly, since my name began with one of those magic letters.

And when, replying to the next question: "Who gave you this name?" I was able to recite confidently, "My sponsors in baptism, wherein I was made a member of Christ, a child of God and an inheritor of the Kingdom of Heaven . . . ("Was that all?" Raymond Sarraute asked in wonderment, when I described my "inheritance")—I had the impression that almost any marvelous and beautiful thing might happen.

What actually did happen was that, every Easter, I wore to church a new white leghorn hat trimmed with field flowers or apple blossoms, and black velvet streamers in back; that on the occasion of one unforgettable Easter march, I was chosen to carry the traditional, large, fern-covered cross into which, after the last triumphant Alleluja had died down, the other marchers stepped forward to insert deep-scented white lilies; that I sang in the vested choir[22] for several years—I roller-skated back and forth to choir practice—and still know the words to countless hymns, the <u>Nunc Dimittis</u>, the <u>Laudate Domini</u> and the <u>Credo</u>. Calvary Episcopal Church being rather high-church, much to my grandmother's disapproval, we bowed our heads in the creed when we pronounced the words: "and in Jesus Christ His only Son our Lord." For her this was "popery," but I felt that it merely showed the proper respect and recognition of the mystery of the Godhead, so I continued to bow my head. For several years too I observed Lent, with its forty days of self-examination and privation ending in the solemn events of Holy Week. Maundy Thursday, the black-draped church of Good Friday, Holy Saturday and finally, Easter, with its promise of Resurrection, were all deeply experienced by me,[23] until . . . well, until I reached the conclusion, some time in my middle "teens," that since the myth was not being lived, it need not be believed. At the time, I did not possess the knowledge that would perhaps have allowed me to see it symbolically against the background of a wider mythology.

As I look back on this period, I am struck by the total absence of any attempt on the part of our parents to influence either our attachment to or detachment from the church. Could it have been that already, skepticism had begun to erode their own belief? Perhaps. In any case, I was the only one of us children for whom the religious experience had significance. Then, one day, almost imperceptibly, I too sloughed it off with few misgivings or regrets. It was as though I had simply outgrown something that naturally, one outgrew. Belief had waned, but many of the reflexes remained, the foundations of a personal ethic which,

22. The choir-master, Frederic Cowles, was also my dearly beloved piano teacher.

23. Many years later, I frequently spoke of these things with Joyce, who was interested to compare the points of agreement and disagreement between the Anglican and the Roman rituals.

while I have seen no other for myself, I have not attempted to impose on the following generations; to teach one must believe. It is as though my life span and personal experience had coincided with the final phases of the historical decline of the Christian influence. If we recall that many of the most atrocious crimes of the XXth Century: Fascism, Nazism, Stalinism, U.S. Imperialism, above all, war and murderous research for further, more devastating wars—have all been committed by predominantly Christian peoples, this impression may be justified.

And yet Christmas, Good Friday, Easter, all those "outward and visible" rituals that quicken an "inner and spiritual grace," are moments without which I believe I would have grown up poorer in spirit.

Chapter III

Curiously enough, although Louisvillians lived in almost complete unawareness of the plastic arts—they had handsome family portraits on their walls, however, and often beautiful original Audubon birds—this was not the case for those who were interested in music. Thanks to a handful of professionals: the organist and choir master, Frederic Cowles, two gifted Leschetitzky-trained pianists, Corneille Overstreet and Julia Whitney, and in a more modest way, to a few talented amateurs, we met together to make our own music: two-piano duets, lieder singing, violin sonatas, etc . . . There were also several music patrons, particularly "Miss Hattie" Speed, with her generously loaned music-room, who could be counted on to support any move to further the cause of good music in Louisville.[24]

Nor was Louisville entirely off-circuit to the nationally active concert bureaux, and before I was 16, I had heard some excellent singing: David Bispham, Marcella Sembrich, Johanna Gadski, Ernestine Schumann-Heink, in the usual repertoire of operatic airs and lieder, were all first-class artists. I have not forgotten either my excitement on hearing the Flonzaley Quartet, at that time Boston's most prestigious string formation, second only to its nationally famous orchestra. Crumbs, all that, but honorable crumbs.

Of course there were few echoes of the important evolution that was taking place in European music at the time: such names as Mussorgsky, Strauss, Schönberg, Webern, Debussy, Stravinsky, even our own Charles Ives, were hardly known. Also, by the time a concert was booked for Louisville, the program was generally limited to well-tried 19th century composers, with, as I recall, a predominance

---

24. There being no concert-hall in Louisville, the concerts usually took place in the Women's Club meeting-room where, on Tuesday afternoons, we also learned to dance under the strict guidance of Miss Mimi Watsdell, shouting "point it! point it!" as she herself, skirts lifted, showed how it was done. Miss Mimi had two prominent, generously hirsute warts on her chin that were irresistibly fascinating to the young.

of Grieg and Tchaikovsky, and an occasional backward dip into the late 18th century. Frequently, for good measure, certain English or American banalities were added. Technically, however, the artists were good, and unless my memory's ear has betrayed me, I believe that their performance could be favorably compared with the best we have known since. Sembrich seems to me to have been an exquisite coloratura, Gadski and Schumann-Heink both fine Wagnerian singers. Unfortunately, recorded music was still very rudimentary so there is probably little evidence to establish these claims other than that of contemporary critics. I should be curious to know what they wrote.

Music was all that for me, of course. I was excited by the formal instruction I was receiving: introduction to the great piano classics, as they became technically accessible, glimpses into the world of opera and lieder. But music was also something very organic. I was listening, charmed, to the beautiful black voices that I heard about me, to their mad, melancholy timbre that was so different from any other, their impeccably subtle, syncopated rhythms. I was trying to sing like them, to enter into their black or brown skins, to discover from within the emotional soil in which this timbre, these rhythms, were rooted. Their hymn-singing, especially: "God be with you till we meet again . . . Till we mee-ee-eet, at Jee-ee-sus's feet," or "There is a fountain filled with blood," with its haunting refrain: "and sinners plunged beneath that flood . . . lose all their guilty stains" . . . which was my first approach to redemption and its terrible price.

From the kitchen and the laundry came complaints that "Maria was always hanging around." This was true. I wanted to listen to their talk and to their singing, to catch their every inflection, which I found infinitely fascinating. Today still, it would be impossible for me to sing, even to recall, that music otherwise than with their intonations, their melancholy passion.

On warm Friday evenings in Spring (there being no school on Saturday) when we gathered together in one another's back-yard, or an a moonlight hay-ride, to sing in harmony to a guitar, or banjo, or mandoline accompaniment—usually all three—we white children too sang a bit sadly and pensively, rarely far from the black mode and mood.

With their contribution to American music, from the cake-walk and minstrel-show days to ragtime, the jug-band, jazz, the blues and rock, the blacks have taught us not only to sing more fervently, but also to dance with entirely new rhythms that have circled the world in this century, making blacks of us all, an event of almost equal importance for the African continent as decolonization itself, if I may indulge in a bit of hyperbole.

❖ ❖ ❖

Any attempt that I might make to give an impartial description of life in Louisville at the beginning of the century would necessarily be incomplete, limited as I was at the time by the tightly stratified social categories I have discussed. We absorbed this truncated reality with our mother's milk, and I should perhaps underline the word 'mother,' (I don't think that Father cared about class distinctions): our daily lives were determined by it, we had practically no other measure of comparison. The city had a population of some 200,000 souls, about one-fifth of whom were black, "our own kind" (we must have been, all told, less than three hundred strong), and "the others," who were identifiable for us to the extent that their reflections appeared in our mirrors. These were the tradespeople, civil servants and numerous professional workers whose activities were as closely imbricated with our lives as ours were with theirs. The relationships were usually friendly and easy-going, but they were not egalitarian, a fact which at the time seemed to disturb no one. It was taken for granted, it was our way of life.

What I shall call the milestone events: births and christenings, graduations and "coming out" parties, engagements and weddings, illness, death . . . were all experiences that were widely shared. What happened to one was the common concern of all and this concern was usually given concrete expression: a gift, flowers; frequently, in case of illness, an especially delicate home-made dish, brought in person in the hope of tempting the invalid appetite.

Except for the débutante balls, the formal dinners and the two principal seasonal events, the autumn horse-show and the late spring racing season, ushered in by the still famous Derby (pronounced Darby, please), the sexes remained separated during the greater part of all this social activity. Husbands and fathers left for their offices shortly after breakfast, they lunched together at their club or in one of the two principal hotels, and did not return until late afternoon. Domestic help being the rule rather than the exception, with the children fed and out of the way, the ladies of the house were free and ready for diversion: afternoon card-parties, formal calls (visiting cards frequently bore such mention as "Tuesday afternoons"), and I recall a letter received by a lady recently returned from Europe, that included the words "Tuesday afternoons" in the address. No doubt before sailing, her card had also borne the three initials P.P.C. [*pour prendre congé,*] which . . . came just after R.S.V.P. in generally accepted visiting-card lore. Finally, there was the card you left in case of absence, your disappointment expressed by a turned-down upper right-hand corner which also showed that you had come in person, that you had not sent the card by a servant. All of which was less complicated probably than the language of flowers, but is hardly, I imagine, a game that will soon be revived. Today I have forgotten which disappeared first, the servant or the card, and once both were gone, this gentle card game collapsed, to be replaced by other less formal conventions, less reassuring, less eloquent of the identity of the players. This was the real game of "lady-come-to-see," the one that, as little girls, we too played for hours at a time, got up like grown ladies in the cast-off skirts, boas and plume or flower-trimmed hats that we fell heir to. We even tried to walk in the old high-heel slippers, holding fast to our sweeping skirts; a fearful delight!

But to return to the separation of the sexes. It can only be explained, I suppose, as a leftover from the days when women were fewer than men in the United States, when their homes and their children, both economically guaranteed by the husband and father, were considered to be their natural and sufficient occupation. But above all, when it was an accepted tenet that a married woman should not be exposed to the charms and temptations of male society, unless her husband were present.[25]

Not that they did not greatly enjoy mixed company, on the contrary. These occasions were generally treated as gala events, and when one of them took place at our house, I remember watching the proceedings with fascination through the upstairs banisters from where, lying flat on the floor, I could see and hear without being seen or heard.

The ladies wore elaborate low-cut evening gowns, the gentlemen dinner coats and black ties, while the table itself, to my eyes, was a glittering maze of immaculate, usually heavily embroidered linen, gold-rimmed goblets, "handsome" china, shining silver, shaded candelabra and flowers. I knew the recent history of all of these items, the preceding days having been given over to cleaning, counting—usually six couples were expected—polishing and shining each object. In addition, floors and furniture had also to be given a mirror-like sheen, windows had to be washed, fresh curtains hung. Already, on the preceding day, the kitchen and pantry regions had begun to be redolent of the most tempting odors. Occasionally, I was allowed to participate in some of the humbler tasks involved: peel mushrooms, or fill little silver dishes with chocolate mints and salted pecans. These moments in the pantry were precious ones to me, because of the atmosphere of gay, eliptical black wit that obtained there, a wit that for subtlety has no equal in my experience.

But as the hours passed, and Mother's nervous tension was obviously rising, I instinctively realized that I would do well to seek as remote a hiding-place as

---

25. From Jordan comes a reminder that those conventions still obtain in certain other societies: ". . . Social life here (in Amman) for men consists mainly of stag parties, political talk and cards, and for women of tea-parties, bridge and charity work. Only occasionally do men and women get together at receptions." <u>Herald-Tribune</u>, May 25, 1978.

possible, usually in the attic, from where I could hear the first guests arrive. This was the signal to come out of hiding, for it meant that Mother was downstairs in the parlor, fulfilling the duties of suave, gracious hostess that she understood so well. The hours that followed more than compensated, probably, for all her pains and tensions. She loved to "entertain."

But what I liked best about these events was the gaiety that they finally engendered. For although the preparations might seem to have suggested an evening at the Court of St. James, this was after all St. James Court, Louisville, and around the table were assembled twelve old friends who had known one another for many years. Once the atmosphere of "best bib and tucker" had worn off, the witty give and take that only fond familiarity can generate took over, and by the time the dessert had arrived, they had started to sing, each guest in turn. This was the moment when Father, as host, was urged to lead off with the only song in his repertoire. "Go on, Don, sing 'The Hebrew Children,'" a humorous ditty of his own composition in which he made hilarious fun of some of the better-known figures in the Old Testament. I remember the verse about the one he called "the bad boy Joshuay."

It began, as all the verses did, with a thrice-repeated query: "Where, oh where, is the bad boy Joshuay?" Then came the answer, sung in chorus by all present: "Way over in the Promised Land." Father continued:

> "Is he a settin' in a chariot of fi-yuh
> Split-crown hat and a red flannel overcoat,
> Tootin' on the curled-up horn of a billy-goat?"

(In chorus) "Wa-a-ay over in the Promised Land," which grew more distant, with greater emphasis on the 'way,' as the song advanced. For there were many more verses, and although Father sang off-key, his obvious pleasure in his own innocent impiety towards these generally revered figures, was contagious. Soon each guest was singing his or her song, grown traditional with the years.

"Miss Clemmie," as Father called Mrs. Jack Woodward (a woman's first name was still a jealously guarded attribute of her 'fair' name), sang her old favorite: "That little old red shawl my mother wore." "It was tattered, it was torn; it showed signs of being worn . . . ," with mock pathos, and as usual, she was warmly applauded. Another feminine guest ventured into romance: "Think of me love tonight, when all the world is still, and in the bright moonlight, trembles each vale and hill . . . ," She went on: "Throw your soft arms about. . . ." They were listening pensively as the song came to an end . . . Sadly, 'twas but a dream." A few seconds elapsed before the chatter started up again.

Finally, when the champagne was served, they raised their glasses right, left and center to the tune of "Come landlord fill the flowing bowl, until it doth run over . . . For tonight we'll merry, merry be . . . ," or perhaps of: "Let every young gentleman fill up his glass!" which ends, I recall, with a "Vive-la, vive-la, vive-l'amour!, vive-la, vive-la, vive-l'amour! (3 times) vive-la, vive-la, vive-l'amour! Vive la compagnie!"

Occasionally, I too was among the singers, summoned by a message brought upstairs by a maid-servant: "Your mama says to wash your face and hands, brush your hair and put on a clean guimpe (a 1940 Webster gives: "a chemisette with sleeves"), then come down and sing for the company."

I had always loved to sing, this was an order I was happy to obey. I usually sang to Mother's barely adequate accompaniment, the first two stanzas of Byron's "To Thomas Moore." The tune, which Mother had taught me, was a simple one that I still like to sing, romantic sadness notwithstanding.

> "My boat is on the shore,
> And my bark is on the sea;
> But before I go Tom Moore,
> Here's a double health to thee!
>
> Here's a sigh to those who love me,
> And a smile to those that hate;
> And, whatever sky's above me,
> Here's a heart for every fate. . . ."

When I had finished singing, after a murmur of approval from the guests—children should not be complimented—my curfew had already sounded: "Say good-night to the company, and go up to bed." It was an order. I obeyed.

❖ ❖ ❖

Theoretically, a young girl, a "filly" (the French *fille* lent itself to use of a term from the horse-breeding world) could be known as "fast"—still in the horse world—indeed, this was considered to be proof, up to a certain point, that she was attractive. It also corresponded to the "wild oats" that both her brother and her future husband were expected to sow during those same years. "We're descended from the Cavaliers, not the Puritans," was the frequent explanation of this indulgence.

An example in retrospect of this "Cavalier" tolerance comes to mind: the permissiveness with which Mother allowed me and some eight or ten neighborhood boys and girls to have our "club" meetings in an unused, isolated top-floor room of our house.

Aged between twelve and fourteen, we were neither children nor adolescents, but in some of us no doubt the sap had already begun to rise. I myself having been provided by nature with an extra skin of indifference to these boys I had always known—an indifference they more than shared—was content to strum the guitar and lead the singing. But others tended to slip naturally into what I shall describe as more than dalliance, but probably less than wantonness. I recall long winter dusks when, after the chatter had died down, and the only light was the glow from the little pot-bellied stove, the only sounds were apt to be murmurs of puppy-love punctuated by an occasional squeal, which I covered with the *continuum* of my guitar. Not that they did not all "marry and live happy ever after." They did. But once married, the girls were supposed to settle down, with eyes for no man but their husbands. And in reality, this was, I think, the way things were, on the surface in any case.

The married women did, however, organize a gyneic world of their own which took the form of gatherings of all kinds: a bridge game, a theatre matinée, discussion clubs, sewing groups, golf, tennis and other such neutral activities that, in season, might also include an afternoon at the races, a swim at the country club, even a baseball game. They were free to do as they liked in fact, as long as the children were well cared for—which they usually were—the house well kept and . . . there were no eligible men involved.

SOME THREE SCORE YEARS AND TEN LATER:

"*L'amour*," Bizet's Carmen has told us for over a century, is "*l'enfant de Bohème*," *un enfant* whose love if unreciprocated, can constitute a threat for its object: "*Prends garde à toi!*" [Watch out!] she warns her soldier lover.

"*L'amour*" is not, however, as Carmen goes on to say, a child that has never been subject to law. On the contrary, physical love and its possible consequences, i.e. progeny and/or disease, have constituted in both primitive and evolved societies, an important concern of social, legal and theological authorities which, by establishing a marriage code, have sought to assure orderly succession of the generations.

Today, in the West, as a corollary to the women's and other "liberation" movements, many of these ancient safeguards have collapsed, and *en avant* for "*l'enfant de Bohème*." No constraints, no sacrifices, no ties that could bind. Life as it will be in Heaven where there is "neither marriage nor giving in marriage," or so we have been promised. Like plastic containers, bed-partners are disposable and disposed of. Sexual promiscuity and deviation, whether inside or outside of marriage, would appear to have lost all trace of punishable transgression.

But life can be very long. That lives which have only shifting sensation to sustain them will reach a dead-end before their time is easily predictable. Sadder still, however, for those who lead them, is the risk of losing that precious attribute: the capacity to care.

There used to be a law on the Kentucky statute books to the effect that any woman, even a hardened prostitute, who had led a life of visible chastity "for a reasonable length of time," could be considered as having regained chastity status, and was therefore subject to rape! A quaint law! Better still, we have since seen a married woman awarded damages for rape by . . . her lawful husband. An epoch-making law!

So let's not despair, equality will come—perhaps. Meanwhile, physical love and its consequences will bear some serious second thoughts on the part of both sexes.

Fortunately for Father, and for us all, his practically one-man undertaking to supply gas, then electricity, to Louisvillians was successful, and the Louisville Gas and Electric company, which he headed until his death in 1924, grew more prosperous as we grew older. So it was possible for me, like Letty and Donald before me, and Cornelia and Angus after me, to have the advantages of a few years' study beyond the provincial cocoon.

After shopping about among various suitable solutions to the problem of chaperonage, Mother enrolled me as a "parlor-boarder," which meant that I would not follow the regular study curriculum, in the Finch School, at 61 East 77th Street in New York City. (Don't forget, gentle reader, that my *SCS* diploma was supposed to have guaranteed me sufficient "book-learning" for life.)[26]

At that time (1909–1910) Finch was the bold modern rival to the very conservative, very exclusive nationally-known school for girls that had been founded earlier in New York by that impeccable preceptress of the hand-picked daughters of hand-picked parents, Miss Spence.

Jessica Garrison Finch who, after a divorce and remarriage had become Jessica Cosgrave, had among other assets, a law degree, and was, I believe, the first of her sex to be admitted to the New York Bar. Her dynamic intelligence undoubtedly injected something into the atmosphere of her school that was probably quite new to the girls' boarding schools, also called "finishing schools," of the time. In 1910 she talked to us of psychology and William James, of economic independence for women, their voting rights and responsibilities, their need for higher education, the *ABC*'s of money and finance, even social injustice.

For beyond the protecting walls that left undisturbed the affluence of the affluent, there was much injustice, much unrest, not only in Europe (what today

26. One day as I was passing by the open door of the English Literature class, I was hailed by the teacher, Kate Thompson: "There goes the ignorant Maria," she told the class good-naturedly, "let's ask her in." But I was hurrying to a piano lesson, so remained alone with my ignorance. Later, she often invited me to her house, suggested books for me to read, and we became excellent friends.

we call the Third World was the concern of businessmen, colonialists and missionaries only), but also in our great cities. An early palliative had been the Neighborhood House movement that had started some twenty years before in Boston, Chicago and on New York's lower east side, the aim of which had been to establish friendly personal contacts that would bridge the gulf of anonymity that separated the social services from those who needed them. But although this formula was adopted in many cities—there were over 400 of these centers functioning throughout the country in 1910—the movement eventually gave way to less personal, perhaps more effective, municipal action.

To her credit, Mrs. Cosgrave was closely associated with an intelligent couple of professional social workers, a Mr. and Mrs. Kelly, whom she encouraged her students to visit and work with whenever possible. The Kellys' deep commitment to sharing the lives of those they were helping, their knowledge of the miserable conditions they were trying to change, provided a salutary contrast to the very comfortable, light-hearted life of the school. Mr. Kelly, I believe, was a native American, while his wife, who spoke English with a marked accent, was of east European origin and had been personally involved with the social and political ferment of the epoch before coming to the United States. It was only natural therefore, given the futile, over-conservative background of many of the pupils, that Mrs. Cosgrave should have left the matter of cooperation with the Kellys to the individual girls and their parents. Suppose they had taken it into their heads to investigate other possible plans for righting social injustice: Socialism, for instance! What then? At that time, the school could not afford to foster subversion.

I was much impressed by my contacts with the Kellys. My own experience in social work thus far had been limited to accompanying Mother on errands for the "Women's Auxiliary" of our church, which consisted mainly as I recall, in distributing Thanksgiving and Christmas dinner baskets to a few worthy poor on "the Point," a neighborhood which, because it was flooded every year by the Ohio river, offered low rents and miserable living conditions. I had also helped the ladies sew for the children in an orphanage called "The Home of the Innocents." (They sewed too for the inmates of a "Home of the Friendless," read "fallen women"—but I was not encouraged to join in this activity). Of course, ever since I could remember, I had been aware that a golden-tongued orator named William Jennings Bryan had attracted Father's passionate support by his valiant attempts to make it impossible for monopolist capitalism to continue to "crucify the workers on a cross of gold." But over the years, Bryan had proved to be a losing candidate and I do not recall that Father ever again gave himself so whole-heartedly to any political figure or party. That "politics" was becoming a dirty affair was generally conceded, and candidates of integrity were becoming rare. However, at the time, people did not seem to foresee that, eventually, honest men's reluctance to seek office would result in a government of *mafiosi*.

◆ ◆ ◆

It is perhaps significant that today in recalling this, my first, cautiously organized sortie outside the native cocoon, I should begin with the impact of ideas on my limited awareness of the world beyond. A strict home discipline and the catechism's injunction to "do my duty in that state of life in which it had pleased God to call me," plus a natural zest for whatever life offered, had created a philosophy of adaptation that left little room for unrest. Life as I found it seemed good. That it was far from good for the large majority of people had remained remote hearsay. Ironically, it was at Finch that the first cracks appeared in the smooth surface of my complacency. A shocking admission? Or a good mark for my parents, who could have wanted their children to attain full growth in order, later, to withstand the "slings and arrows" that, encountered too young, could maim? The truth probably was simply that we lived in a time and a place in which the legitimacy of traditional class demarcations was still unquestioned. We did not feel concerned. The class war with its strikes and bombs, was going on elsewhere: in Europe, and sporadically in such places as Chicago, the West Virginia mines, the Pennsylvania steel communities. In any case it did not concern us. The South had only recently known great violence and suffering. Its people were finally able to forget, to live their genteel lives in peace. Was this a crime? Not that such rationalizations were ever actually formulated. But if the prevailing smugness had been challenged I don't doubt that they would have been.

The two Finch years (1909 to 1911) were rich as well in new experiences. Piano lessons with Elizabeth Strauss, one of Leschetitzky's most gifted pedagogues, were for me a revelation, not only musically but intellectually. She was implacable in her insistence that practise which did not involve absolutely concentrated effort, was of no value, and she was quick to recognize when this condition had not been met. She also insisted that my musical horizon should be broadened, and took me with her to many excellent concerts including those that Gustav Mahler conducted for the New York Philharmonic Orchestra during his 1909–1910 visit to the States.

In addition to these concerts the school organized parties to the opera. On these occasions we wore our very best evening dresses with matching slippers and, accompanied by a dignified duenna, drove the forty city blocks from East 77th Street to the Metropolitan Opera House in a horse-drawn carriage with upholstered benches for 3 on either side.

Those were the Puccini years: <u>Madame Butterfly</u>, <u>La Tosca</u>, <u>La Vie de Bohème</u>, <u>The Girl of the Golden West</u>, were frequently staged, and we heard them all, usually with Geraldine Farrar and Enrico Caruso in the leading roles. At that time Caruso was also starring to wildly enthusiastic audiences in Leoncavallo's "Pagliacci." How he could break your heart and make the great Metropolitan chandeliers tremble with his "Ride, Ridi, Pagliaccio!" To say that we had a collective crush on Caruso would be a vast understatement.

But there were other gods and goddesses of the opera, particularly goddesses: the famous Emma Calvé in <u>Carmen</u>; beautiful Lina Cavallieri in the <u>Contes d'Hoffmann</u>, singing "<u>Belle Nuit, O Nuit d'Amour,</u>" as she toured a cardboard Venice in a cardboard gondola; corpulent, angel-voiced Emmy Destinn in <u>Rigoletto</u>; Tetrazzini, Melba . . . they were all there, and many others as well. One fly in our ointment, however, when, as inevitably happened, after each Caruso triumph some old opera-goer seated nearby, would sigh and say, "Ah, but you see I heard Jean de Reszke."[27]

◆ ◆ ◆

One last memory of Finch. On soft spring afternoons when for lack of a garden, the girls drifted up to the roof: lots of freshly shampooed hair drying in the sun; scattered here and there, deck chairs occupied by totally absorbed readers, lost probably in the sensuous, magnificently told stories of George Moore's heroines, Evelyn Inness or Esther Waters. At that time, for the young, Moore was decidedly "caviar," rather naughty "caviar" at that, and his books were passed eagerly from hand to hand.

There would have been too a little knot of singers: the <u>Pink Lady</u> waltz, Fritzi Scheff's <u>Every Little Movement</u> which, we recall, "has a meaning all its own," or <u>The Girl on the Saskatchewan</u>. And as far as one could see, Manhattan: to the east, the poor streets and avenues leading to the East River; to the West, pompous Fifth Avenue, Central Park, the prosperous Upper West Side and far beyond, the Hudson which, for most of us, was not only Rip Van Winkle's beautiful, wide stream that bordered the island on its way to the Atlantic. It was also the recognizable line of demarcation between the great metropolis to which we had been sent and the vast hinterland from which we had come, to which we would return. Beyond the Hudson, lay home.

If I had been gifted with clairvoyance—but I was not—I might have sensed the wretched presence on those West Side streets of the newly arrived young Lorraine immigrant, Eugene Jolas, whom I was to marry some fifteen years later. But it would have taken a bold astrologer indeed to make this prediction in 1910. Propinquity is not necessarily communication.

---

27. So did Joyce and in the same role. He concluded that de Reszke had the same timbre as his father, John Stanislas Joyce.

❖ ❖ ❖

I was to spend two more years in New York. Not at Finch, however, but in what was quaintly called a "chaperone home" for out-of-town students. This one occupied a small brown-stone house near Washington Square and the "chaperone" was an intelligent, eminently respectable New England lady, Miss Caroline Lewis. Her household consisted of four girls and one boy, aged sixteen, her nephew, Dwight Fiske, who was studying composition. Dwight was by far the most talented among us and today, a numerous public on both sides of the Atlantic will recall that he had a long, active career as a highly sophisticated "entertainer" who created his own inimitable medium: seated at the piano, he told one hilariously funny story after another (his humor was of the dry, acerbic kind) while playing an equally witty, always brilliantly composed, accompaniment. Already, in our student days, he used to amuse himself—and us—by his piano portraits which kept us, as the saying went, "in stitches."

Where are they now? Dwight, I know, died some time ago. As for the others, the sixty odd years that have passed since we were together under Miss Lewis's chaperonage, have effaced all traces.

❖ ❖ ❖

It was a very pleasant time to be living in New York, especially in that part of the city which, after having been neglected and allowed to run down for some years, was beginning to attract a population that welcomed the quiet gentility, the occasional tree or back yard, that the old, patinated houses offered. Also, a breeze of excitement was beginning to blow through Washington Square as artists and poets descended from their low-priced lofts to exchange ideas, show their work, read their poems or like lazy lizards just bask in the sun. Soon uptowners, hearing about these signs of life, grew curious and came down to take a look. The neighborhood bard, guitar-playing, ditty-singing Bobby Edwards—the Bob Dylan of 1910—had the following lyrical comment to make on these incursions:

> "Way down yonder in Greenwich village
> Where they get the uptown spillage,
> Where the interior decorators
> Flirt with the clerks from Wanamaker's . . ."
> etc.

There were many more verses and Bobby's owl-like face, his quick sense of new expressions and topical allusions made him a favorite in the little eating-places that began to mushroom. "Interior decorators" was a newly coined name, a direct ancestor of "realtor" and "beautician," while Wanamakers had only recently moved down-town. It was fun to hear them juxtaposed. But this was mere foam on the stein.

An event of historical importance had taken place in September 1909 when Freud, Jung, and Breuer met with their American colleagues at Clark University, in Worcester, Massachusetts.[28]

At that meeting an element was injected into the national bloodstream that was gradually to dissolve the very source of the American ethic: Puritanism. Indeed, the havoc wrought by the visit of these "bearers of the pest" (their own description) eventually left no single institution untouched. But that the dynamite of what was being discussed in Worcester should have been sufficiently potent to penetrate the awareness of such innocent by-standers as the girl-students at Finch, is still a source of wonder to me. And I remember my surprise when, on arriving in Paris ten years later, I discovered that most French people had not only never heard of psychoanalysis, but were quite indifferent to attempts to interest them in its fascinating new methods of exploration. "French people know how to live," was the most frequent comment, "they don't need that kind of thing!"

I myself am inclined to think that they "had something" there. The all-embracing Code-Napoleon, along with the other hierarchies, was still functioning, apparently satisfactorily, in spite of the recent war upheaval. A man was still *chef de famille,* his wife, who knew her place, was crowned *mère de famille*—a noble title!—by Church and state alike, children did as they were told, or else . . . It was still, or so it seemed to me, a no-nonsense society in which the marginal remained on the margin. When people dreamed and the dream was sufficiently irrational in their eyes, they might tell it for this reason, otherwise dreams were apt to be dismissed and forgotten. As for that delicious *volupté,* confession, for the large majority of the, at that time, usually Catholic French, it was confined to priestly ears.

That this Viennese "pest" would eventually worm itself into the French consciousness was of course inevitable, and indeed the schisms and anti-schisms of the process are still (1976) a permanently exciting feature of the perennial *film à épisodes* of Parisian intellectual life. But the powerful opposition of Medical

---

28. The Boston neurologist, James J. Putnam (1846–1916) who, since 1894, had been following the work of Freud and other European experimenters, was largely responsible for this meeting. His old friend, William James, who, also in 1894, had written on the Freud-Breuer hysteria findings, went to Worcester for the event "to see what Freud was like." In a letter to Putnam dated August 8, 1910, Freud described himself as a "God-forsaken, incredulous Jew."

chauvinism, of the Catholic Church, then of the Communist Party, constituted a serious rampart that left the French public in a state of psychoanalytical innocence until after the Second World War.[29] Heretics might comment, "lucky French." Far be it from me to say, I personally seem to have been vaccinated early in life against the maladies for which this therapy was recommended. But no doubt, if I were to look more closely, I would find that the unavoidable process of acculturation had nevertheless deposited in me a fair number of psychoanalytical attitudes the very source of which has been lost to sight. So much for the pore-penetrating *Zeitgeist*. But I seem to be shamelessly anticipating. Let's return to 1912.

On the heels of the great literary movement of social protest that had been gathering momentum and talent in the Middle West ever since the appearance of Theodore Dreiser's Sister Carrie (1900),[30] an equally important poetic revival that was to dominate the first half-century had also begun to make itself felt.[31] Amy Lowell's Poetry, Harriet Monroe's Poetry a Magazine of Verse, Floyd Dell's and Max Eastman's The Masses, provided modern, socially oriented vehicles (particularly The Masses), for this new poetry which one critic, Amos Wilder,[32] later described as "ethically-grounded."

Not that I myself at that time was very aware of the significance of these new writers for the evolution of the America literary consciousness. I was still in the Spanish Inn stage: "you find in it what you bring to it," still lacked the special antennae required to capture these waves. In fact I believe that I read The Masses more for its social than its literary content. My primary esthetic interest was still music.

But here, too, important things were happening. Not so much in America; by 1912 although Charles Ives had written some of his most revolutionary works, since none of them was performed before 1920, the Concord Sonata not until 1939! We did not know that one of America's major composers had been aroused and inspired at the same time and by the same seeding wind that had

---

29. There were of course brilliant exceptions: André Breton, Theodore Frankel and other future surrealists, to mention only this group, as early as 1916, were aware of psychoanalysis.

30. For the record, *the novelists:* Frank Norris, b. 1870, Theodore Dreiser, b. 1871, Jack London, b. 1876, Sherwood Anderson, b. 1876, Upton Sinclair, b. 1878, Sinclair Lewis, b. 1885, John Dos Passos, b. 1890 etc.

31. *The poets:* Edgar Lee Masters b. 1869, E.A. Robinson b. 1869, E.E. Cummings b. 1874, Amy Lowell b. 1876, Robert Frost b. 1875, Carl Sandburg b. 1878, Wallace Stevens b. 1879, Vachel Lindsay b. 1879, W.C. Williams b. 1883, Sara Teasdale b. 1884, Ezra Pound b. 1885, Louis Untermeyer b. 1885, Marianne Moore b. 1887, T.S. Eliot b. 1888.

32. "Spiritual Aspects of the New Poetry," Harper's, New York, 1940.

blown through the ranks of the poets and novelists. Much later, it amused me to identify for my composer daughter, Betsy, and her friends, a theme that Ives used in "Central Park in the Dark" as being simply the tin-pan alley ditty that had inaugurated the introduction of the telephone into American life:

> Hello, ma honey, hello ma baby,
> Hello ma ragtime gal,
> Send me a kiss by wire . . ."

I forget if Ives used the ending, which after a few tritely rhymed lines about love and life ends: "Hello! Hello! Hello! there."

What we did know however, but from afar, was that Debussy's Pelléas and Mélisande was already ten years old,[33] that in 1912 Pierrot Lunaire was given in Berlin, and Ravel's Daphnis et Chloé in Paris, where gradually we were to learn that Apollinaire, Reverdy, Proust, Picasso, Matisse and their friends were already laying the foundations of a new esthetic that would inspire the creators for another half-century.

Chapter IV

ANTE-BELLUMS

How did it happen that you were allowed to go alone to Berlin to study singing? This question has occasionally been asked me, somewhat to my surprise. Unlike their brothers, for whom the age of "majority" was 21, southern girls were considered to be "of age" at 18. In 1913 I was 20 years old, I could, I should in fact, have been married and starting to raise a family. But since there was no sign of this solution, why not music in Europe? A combination of apparently unrelated small events quite unpredictably paved the way for my departure for Berlin.

At the heart of these events was, of course, my own musical evolution. In addition to piano lessons, while in New York I had started singing lessons, with little enthusiasm for my teacher, however, from whom I soon separated. But this latter fact in no way kept me from singing, or dampened my ambition to become a real singer, possibly even, an opera singer!

At the Metropolitan Opera House, with a camp-stool and sufficient gumption to get an early place in the waiting line, you could stand in the *promenoir* for $1.00. I had heard practically the entire repertoire, from Il Trovatore, Aida, and the Puccini operas, which were great favorites, to Parsifal, the Ring and

---

33. Joyce paid 7.50 francs to hear it during its first season, no doubt with Mary Garden as Mélisande.

Tristan. But although I had cut my opera-fan's teeth on the Italians, I had gradually come to feel that Wagner was the greatest of them all, and I think that I must have heard all of his operas many times. (Curiously enough, I recall hearing little Mozart and only an occasional Carmen). For New York audiences of that time, opera was either Italian or German. I decided, although I knew literally no German, that with determination and tenacity, I would learn the role of Isolda by rote with no other aid than a dictionary.

Just here chance oriented my compass eastward when Mother decided that we would spend the next summer vacation in Warm Springs, a pre-1860 summer-resort in the Virginia mountains. There I met a Baltimore singer, George Gibson, with whom I passed many hours singing duets, accompanying him, or just talking excitedly about music. His two grown daughters were gay and congenial, Mrs. Gibson was immensely hospitable, the Gibson cottage soon became my favorite haunt.

Warm Springs! And I don't mean Hot Springs which, while it was only ten miles away, was the meeting place of an entirely different kind of human species: affluent northerners and European visitors, about whom we provincially noted that if they themselves seemed to have little zest for life (not our kind, in any case), they usually owned dogs and horses that did. For us, the Hot Springs was a place we visited occasionally, to drink tea on the lawn of the "Homestead" Hotel, with its striped parasols and afternoon band-concerts, or to avail ourselves of the more sophisticated shopping facilities than existed in our end of the valley.

"The Warm," on the other hand, was so different, so familiarly southern, that it could almost have been our own creation. The always starchily white-clad old lady who presided over its comforts and pleasures, Mrs. Talulla Eubank—"Miss Tew" to the thirty or more black employees—was herself an ante-bellum figure whose eye, invisible like God's, saw all, even though she rarely left her private quarters on the hill behind the hotel, to which few were summoned except those responsible for the well-being of her two hundred or so guests. Once, on some special errand, I was admitted into the presence, and had time to note with ill-concealed curiosity that the lines of matching medicine bottles on open shelves beside her rocker, bore no names other than those of the indispositions they were supposed to relieve, headache, back-ache, stomach-ache, tooth-ache, etc.

The hotel proper was a large white frame building with right and left curving stairs leading on to a wide veranda that ran the length of the house, and on which was a long line of white hickory rocking-chairs. A vast dining-room at one end, and a "ball-room" at the other, between which were offices and card-rooms, occupied the main floor. On the two upper floors were the bed-rooms. Very tall, old trees, surrounded by well-tended lawns and flower-beds, enhanced the look of genteel age, as did a dozen or so one-storey whitewashed brick cottages strung out on either side of the walk, to the left of the entrance. Year after year, the same multi-coloured hollyhocks, the same hydrangeas, the same bright, pungent phlox, bloomed against the freshly whitened walls.

The summer guests too had something perennial about them: the names of forebears, who had stopped there a century earlier, were often still to be found on the old registers, with occasional mention of the quantity and cost of the libations they had consumed.

But here was not only a monument to the past. After all, the place was called "Warm Springs," which name had not been idly chosen. The sulphur springs were still flowing, still warm; the days were still centered around your dip in one of the roofed-over pools (one for the ladies and one for the gentlemen), easily accessible down gently sloping footpaths, and presided over by elderly blacks of matching sex who dried the towels and decorous bathing garments, in addition to beating the backs of the bathers as they came out of the pool, to prevent possible chill. This routine made for considerable bathrobe migration between the cottages. It also broke whatever ice could have withstood the hot Virginia summers; people quickly came to know one another, the atmosphere was congenial and friendly.

This essential rite accomplished, the rest of the day and much of the night, for the younger guests, were devoted to what I shall call the three "F's": flirtation, frivolity and food.

Under the first of these headings there were sub-headings, principal among them: buggy-riding for two, in a two-seat horse-drawn vehicle, over little-frequented woodland roads that lent themselves to mutual revelation. My own initiation into this exquisite experience was marred, alas, by the fact that though I was kissed on the cheek and marriage was proposed, this first candidate for life partnership proved to be so incurably oafish that having weakly said yes, I quickly said no.

Next came the less costly but equally soul-revealing pastime, also for two, which we called "bush-whacking," i.e. that long walk in the woods, *à deux,* when you denuded a switch of its leaves and, for emphasis, or simply to fill the silence, "whacked" the bordering vegetation.

There was also, of course, daily horse-back riding, still for two, the girls riding side-saddle, over shady woodland bridle paths.

Finally, in the evening, after a copious supper, as that meal was called, we usually drifted towards the casino porch for dancing to gramophone records. For like any self-respecting spa, the Warm Springs Hotel had a nearby frame building dubbed "the casino," with a bar, card tables and a wide veranda for moonlight dancing, close harmony, and/or spooning, which today may have a more specific name.

Occasionally, weather and the moon permitting, we picnicked on "flag rock," a famous civil-war lookout-post, an hour's walk to the top of the nearest mountain. Supper usually consisted of the traditional eggs and bacon, cooked over an open fire, with potatoes roasted in the coals, and watermelon for dessert.

After this rarely-varied meal, a mood of singing and dreaming set in, as we watched the moon rise over the blue-hazed ridges and valleys that, as far as the eye could see, occupied the landscape. Hand-holding couples seated around the fire, stared, fascinated, into the flames.

But before you could say "Jack Robinson," it was midnight. Time to pack up and start the tired-but-happy trek down.

◆ ◆ ◆

By noon, the elderly ladies, who were more numerous than their male counterparts, having recovered from the exertions of the warm, sulphur bath, had begun to take possession of the white rockers on the veranda. They were usually dressed in crisp, ruffly white, grey or lavender, the progression away from the black decreed for widows. Their pale touched-up hair released from its curlers, and their pale cheek-bones "touched-up" with a dab of not always discreetly applied rouge (one wore the smooth dead-white plaster coating associated with paintings of Japanese prostitutes), like birds that have bathed and dusted their wings, they soon began to converse animatedly: about ancestors and descendants, marriage and rumored adultery, (divorce was still rare), fortunes made and lost, babies born and unborn, servants—always an inexhaustible topic—and that most fascinating of all: their own experiences of childbirth and surgery. This was the very stuff of life, absorbing, an occupation that lent itself to the most intimate analysis and comment. Occasionally, a little tell-tale puddle could be seen under one of the chairs, but eyes turned quickly aside and this phenomenon was studiously ignored.

With the arrival of the elderly gentlemen, after a quick review of the more salient events of the day, (the transistor was not yet a possible *vade mecum*), they soon settled down to discussion of the late war (1861–1865) and its aftermath. No other people west of Suez, probably, unless it be Turgeniev's country squires, were ever greater talkers than those aging southerners on vacation, although I have read from the pen of Richard Ellmann that the Irish claim to be the greatest talkers since the Greeks. Could it be that defeat loosens the tongue? Yet, come to think of it, French people are every bit as garrulous as we are. In fact, they have added something specifically French to garrulity, that can attain to virtuosity: they are perfectly capable of carrying on a two-, even a three-tiered simultaneous conversation without missing a word of what has been said, a form of communication that, while it can become pretty deafening for bystanders, has at least the virtue of discouraging monologue.

Having described flirtation and frivolity as practised by the young and, to a lesser extent, by the very old, what, one might ask, were the occupations and concerns of the solid middle-aged? The answer is simple: between solid meals, they played solid bridge and drank solid mint-juleps, the wine of the country. Except for an occasional post-mortem analysis of the day's game, garrulity was not their affair. The dining-room might buzz, as the white-coated black waiters served a mid-day meal composed of soup, at least three baked meats and at times, as many as six vegetables, rarely were the bridge-fiends among the noise-makers. Their thoughts were on the game, that lost rubber should have been played differently. They would adopt another strategy next time.

◆ ◆ ◆

Some time in August, our little band of bush-whacking, flirting, buggy-riding young people organized a mixed bathing-party in one of the pools, with candle-lighted trays of drinks and sandwiches floating on the slightly odorous, because sulphurous, water. This event, which sent some eyebrows upward, usually pre-saged the summer's approaching end, those who lingered on through the cool September fortnight, when the Hotel closed, being reduced thereafter for entertainment to such bucolic activities as hunting mushrooms—the big field variety—which, creamed on toast, for a chafing-dish supper, added variety to the classic egg and welsh-rarebit menus. And always the singing, always the gay banter.

"Where is now that merry party?" The old song supplies its own response: "They are all dispersed and wandered, far away—far away . . ."

◆ ◆ ◆

The final event of the Warm Springs season was the late August "ball" held in the rarely used "ball-room," with music furnished by a three-piece orchestra imported from "The Hot." This was a community affair made possible by each guest's cooperation: we bush-whackers gathered the many yards of "sweet, southern smilax" that festooned the ball, while Miss Tew provided refreshments and service. Best of all, the entire black personnel joined together to "walk" for the cake, which was the main feature of the evening's entertainment.

Like the rest of us, they were dressed in their brightest and best, and after they had walked solemnly around the hall with beautiful suppleness, the most spectacular high-stepping couple was awarded the specially-baked cake, by a jury chosen among the guests.

Is it merely wishful reminiscing on my part, or did this moment of grace really break down the last color barriers for the rest of the evening? Did we really all dance together after that blessed interval? It seems to me that we did, I hope that we did, (I fear that we did not).

◆ ◆ ◆

My daughter Tina comments on this chapter that my presentation of that summer vacation is surely not the way it actually was; that it could not have been as lighthearted and idyllic as, in retrospect, I have recalled it. But it was! At least it was for me.

Remember the date: summer 1913, and the place: a miraculously preserved, self-contained little ante-bellum Virginia community, set in a gently desuet natural paradise. I myself was seeing life through the eyes of my 20 years. I was still, for reasons too many to analyze here, a total stranger to the disturbing preoccupations of the "tender passion." I was simply relishing the presence of these congenial new friends, the patinated beauty of the old place.

If our hedonist elders were aware that summer of the threat of war in Europe, there was no sign of it. Europe was a ten-day ocean-voyage away, almost an alien planet, to which few Southerners, who were still relatively poor, could afford to travel. I believe that for these children of the Civil War, our parents, this was a charmed moment, during which they too doffed their winter cares and enjoyed to the full the lazy, ecstatic summer days that only too quickly would be gone.

(History recalls that five years later, the terrible blood-letting in Europe finally ended, an obscure German philosopher-historian published a disturbing book entitled "Decline of the West").

"And that," as French people wittily say when an over-elaborate elucidation fails to elucidate, "is why your daughter is a deaf-mute."

Actually, these homely vacation notes are indispensable to what was to follow. For but for that Warm Springs summer I don't believe that I would have gone to Berlin to study singing. Long hours of singing and music-making with George Gibson, his warm encouragement and the audition he arranged for me in his native Baltimore with the Director of the Peabody Conservatory of Music, —who gave me a letter of recommendation to the famous Lilli Lehmann— convinced my parents that I should seriously study singing, and that Germany was the best place for me to do so. They generously made it possible.

Once this decision had been taken, a few enquiries revealed that a friend of our family, Agatha Bullitt of Louisville, who had married a German, was living in Berlin and would be happy to have me board with them, which greatly facilitated my plans.

Thus it was that one night early in November, 1913, following an evening at a Manhattan theatre, I boarded the Norddeutscher Lloyd steamer IMPERATOR. After a supper-party on board for friends who had come to see me off, at one a.m., the great liner began to move gently out to sea. I was carrying no passport, no identity papers of any kind, in fact, except a steamship ticket made out in my name. Today, this hardly seems credible when one reflects on the suspicious, bureaucratic tyranny that, less than one year later, had assumed tight control, and still holds sway over our international movements.

I remember very little about the ten-day voyage, which passed in a happy haze of time-killing activities: the rite of hot bouillon served on deck in mid-morning, while a brass band did its *umpah, umpah* best to entertain the deck-walkers, solitary and in twos; the permanent card-games in the smoking room; the excitement of the Captain's dinner which preceded the farewell "fancy-dress" ball, not forgetting the many ripening romances; all features that have since disappeared from trans-Atlantic travel, time having become "of the essence," air having replaced water.

One morning, finding myself alone in the company of a sailor who was scrubbing the deck, I tried to enter into conversation with him. My German being limited to my memory of Isolda's first dialogue with Tristan, I addressed the young man by the familiar pronoun "Du." He beat an embarrassed retreat.

❖ ❖ ❖

Ten days later, Agatha Grabisch's friendly smile greeted me from the Bremen dock, and after a short train-ride, I had taken possession of my room in the third-floor flat of the *gartenhaus* at 48 Knesebeckstrasse, in the Charlottenberg quarter of West Berlin.

The household consisted of Agatha, her husband Jo Grabisch, a keen, smiling, "rough diamond" sort of man, who was apparently in close touch with the still subversive action of the Expressionists. (It was through him that I first heard the name of Carl Einstein, who had just published his hilariously acid <u>Bebuqpuin</u>, which Jo quoted with glee). Next came my somewhat intimidated self and, finally, a very loud-singing, blousy *Dienstmädchen* named Emma, from whom I learned several of the more ribald songs of the time. <u>Die Männer sind alle Verbrecher</u> . . . <u>aber lieb, aber lieb sind sie doch</u>!, appeared to be her motto. But Emma remains closely identified with those first Berlin days for another, more dramatic reason.

"We shall go out for supper," Agatha told me one evening shortly after my arrival, "since Emma is not well and a doctor has been called." When I walked into the kitchen a few minutes later, the Doctor had already arrived and was washing his hands over the sink with unusual care. Summoning with difficulty my very elementary German, I succeeded in formulating the question: *Ist-sie sehr krank?* Without looking at me, the doctor let fly the reply: *Sie hat ein Kind.* Whew! In spite of having experienced in my own family, the arrival (in cabbages?) of a sister, then a brother, this was the nearest I had ever come to childbirth. There was a mother and her new-born child in that windowless little room off the kitchen! I was awed.

Emma's story was dark and banal, an illustration of her song. One of several witnesses, Jo Grabisch had jumped into the Spree to rescue her from attempted suicide. But it was what followed the birth that I found impressive. For there took place a minutely executed paternity search—all the men she was known to have frequented however remotely, within the prescribed time limit, were questioned, German law at the time requiring that a child born out of wedlock should be brought up according to the financial circumstances of the father. Emma's case was not limpidity itself, however, and I fear that her son did not move into the category the French call "social promotion." Quite evidently too she had been "betrayed" by one of her own. The baby was placed in the care of her large peasant family and a week later, the young mother was back at work, singing her worldly-wise songs.

Emma showed me a group photograph of her family which intrigued me: one of the brothers who appeared hardly to be aware of his siblings, was staring at something that the others evidently did not see. Emma explained: "Oh, that brother died before the picture was taken, so his photograph had to be added."

Emma's baby, no doubt, had a warm nest to grow up in. Just in time, poor devil, to shout "Heil Hitler!"

◆ ◆ ◆

Berlin, 1913. An ominous date. But I did not know the word ominous. In my far-off Kentucky home, I had been blissfully unaware of the European rumblings that, for the initiated, no doubt foretold the immense drama about to unfold. I had no knowledge of the background events that would have permitted me to understand. I was simply taking in the new city through my pores, my eyes, my ears.

I remember my astonishment at seeing in the *Tiergarten,* in late November, a lovely pink rose in full bloom. Astonishment because, in Louisville, that rosebush would have bloomed so permanently through the scorching summer months that, by November, it would have long since ceased to bloom. This gave me some understanding of Berlin's latitude, of the increasingly early nightfall; then, towards winter's end, of the rapidly lengthening days. All of these things I experienced as new and different.

There were others: the very special, sweetish odour of the fuel used in German automobiles. Re-encountering that smell many years later, brought back those first Berlin days more vividly than anything I might have seen or heard.

Principally, however, the sound of the new language was both exciting and frustrating. I was making a great effort to learn it, and Agatha Grabisch, who was an experienced teacher, gave me a lesson every day. I remember that we soon plunged into a German translation of <u>Peer Gynt</u> which, in addition to hearing German at meals (Jo spoke no English), helped to familiarize me with the idiomatic spoken language. I imagine that it was many weeks, however, before I was anything more than an eager listener during the informal evenings that were a feature of the Grabisch household that winter. The tall young American woman was a subject of curiosity on the part of the guests. Why had she come to Berlin? "She hopes to become a singer, perhaps even an opera-singer," Grabisch explained with a smile. I have not forgotten the comment of an older man who, I realized, had been looking me over. "*Die Figur hat sie schön,*" he remarked. I pondered this word. What kind of *Figur* should an opera-singer have?

Soon, as I became better acquainted with the neighbourhood, I discovered other possibilities of hearing German, among them, attendance at Church.

At the entrance to the nearby broad *Kurfürstendamm,* there was a large, unbeautiful 19th century church: the *Kaiser-Wilhelm Gedächtnisskirche,* which shared the popular *Kaiser-Wilhelm Platz* with two more mundane institutions: the *Kaffee des Westens,* a spacious, always crowded caravanserai, where we often joined a *stammtisch*[34] of friends, and the *Kaufhaus des Westens,* a bustling department store. The church being within easy walking distance of the Knesebeckstrasse, I became a frequent worshipper there well before I could intelligibly follow the service. The sermons particularly, which were long and earnest, I simply let drench me, until gradually certain words—the word *arbeit,* for instance—began to have meaning for me. This word was usually accompanied by other members of its semantic family, it was an ever-recurring theme: *arbeit, arbeiter, arbeiten, gearbeitet,* and I soon came to believe the truth of the familiar saying according to which "Germans do not work to live, they live to work."

During World War II, the *Kaiser-Wilhelm Gedächtniss Kirche* was heavily bombed, and seemed doomed to disappear along with many other Berlin landmarks. Pious souls, however, opposed a plan to raze the ruin and build a new church. Instead, the remaining walls were consolidated, vines were planted, and today it stands, a gaunt, ugly, though vine-clad symbol of an ugly, terrible time.

---

34. The witty *stammtisch* guests grouped these three landmarks together under the irreverently rhymed sobriquet: "*Kauf* haus des Westens, *Sauf* haus des Westens and *Tauf* haus des Westens"—*kauf*en, to buy; *sauf*en, to guzzle, *tauf*en, to baptise.

❖ ❖ ❖

Church, then, as a place to hear the language well spoken. Other less didactically beneficial, but nevertheless instructive possibilities, were the conversations necessitated by visits to shops, both large and small. However, I recall my chagrin in the *Kaufhaus des Westens* when, having painfully formulated my question: "*Wo sind Damen Hüte?*" I realized that I had not understood a word of the reply. After an effusive "*Danke sehr,*" I walked straight ahead, but did not that day find the ladies' hat department.

On another occasion, in a small glove-shop, I was able to penetrate well beyond mere buyer-and-seller dialogue into the very heart of a certain social mentality, how typical of the time I would be unable to say.

Kaiser Wilhelm II had been on the throne since 1890, and his heir, the *Kronprinz* was now ready to assume the rôle of Kaiser, should the succession fall open. The 20th Century was in its second decade, the image the prince sought to project was that of modernity. A constantly visible example of this feature of the future ruler was his presence on the streets of Berlin, at the wheel of a dashing sports-car, equipped with a very loud Klaxon, unlike that of any other in the city: *do si! do fa!*

As I held up my hand to permit the saleswoman to fit the glove, while she gently smoothed each finger into its sheath, the familiar klaxon sounded loud and clear in a nearby street; the woman's frown of concentration gave way to a beaming smile: "*Ach! unser Kronprinz!*" she murmured with fond indulgence. There were many of her kind, probably, who would have liked to see that prosperous, Prussianized régime pursue its ambitious, smugly Biedermeier course. They failed to reckon with the threat that the Expressionists and Spartakists from within, and Allied suspicions from without, would constitute for the National edifice they so confidently regarded as "*Deutschland über Alles.*"

❖ ❖ ❖

Shortly after my arrival, Agatha announced that it was high time for us to go *stempeln*, which was the familiar verb for submitting one's identity papers to the police for their rubber-stamp of approval. She explained that this was an administrative requirement for my continued presence in the country.

But what identity papers? My steamship ticket? Certainly not, was the official reply. I must show a passport *and* a birth certificate, neither of which yet existed in the United States arsenal of required diplomatic documents. As the great man said: "*que faire?*"

I wrote home for advice. Father was shocked. How was it possible that his daughter should have to be brought in contact with the German police? His first reaction was to urge me to return to America. Agatha wrote to explain that it was an official formality applicable to all foreign visitors, most of whom had been provided with these papers by their governments.

The police began to sympathize with my predicament. "There must be some record, some witness of the date and circumstances of your birth," the clerk insisted. Finally, a Kentucky relative, my dear Aunt Amelia, who was also my godmother, agreed to testify that in 1893 she had held me over the baptismal font of Calvary Episcopal Church in Louisville, Kentucky, where, fortunately, the necessary vital statistics had been recorded in the Parish baptismal register. Her letter to this effect, duly witnessed, satisfied the requirements of the Berlin police; I would be allowed to stay.

Today, this verb *stempeln,* which has remained so closely associated in my mind with that 1913 incident, has come to symbolize for me the all-powerful bureaucracies that keep jealous watch over both sides of national frontiers, harassing and discouraging would-be travelers.

Once, it seems to me, we Americans had a different vision. Our gates were open, people were innocent until they had been proved guilty. Let them come!

But the legal imperative of obtaining a governmental document of identity before leaving one's country (introduced into international life, I am told, by Turkey and Russia), with the many vexations that this can entail, was to cross the Atlantic sooner, than we thought, the result of the traumatizing events of 1914–1918 in Europe. I myself have never again traveled in a state of such diplomatic innocence as I did on the IMPERATOR.

◆ ◆ ◆

After the *Polizei,* my next urgent visit was to Lilli Lehmann, in order personally to deliver the letter from the Director of the Peabody Institute and, if she agreed to take me, arrange for lessons.

I recall a tall, handsome woman with beautiful, well-groomed white hair. Very stately, a bit forbidding even, her personality was in marked contrast to the *petit bourgeois* atmosphere of her little suburban house. I was all the more struck by this contrast, because the importance of Lilli Lehmann, her long and brilliant operatic career, were things I had known before leaving America. I remember, too, being childishly fascinated during that brief visit to observe that although the great diva was wearing a handsome silk blouse, it had been patched under both arms—very neatly patched, in fact—with two non-matching silk pieces. Could she have fallen on hard times? Or was this just *hausfraulich* frugality? I never knew.

Sadly for me, after reading the Baltimore letter, Lehmann explained to Frau Grabisch that no matter who recommended a new pupil, she could accept no more, and gave us the address of her assistant. My disappointment was immense. But I realized later that her refusal was perhaps my good fortune. For like many great singers, Lehmann's analysis of her own "method," to judge by her assistant's teaching and also by her own book, <u>Mein Weig</u> (in English, <u>How to Sing</u>), was less than helpful. I fear too, that during the months I worked with the assistant, I did not make the progress I had hoped for. But that was a time when the art of teaching singing seemed to many to have been lost; one could only conjecture that the difficult vocal scores of the 18th and early 19th centuries must have been written for singers capable of singing them. This was one of the reasons why I had been encouraged to study with an older singer who, herself, had been trained in the *bel canto* technique of past generations.

Almost miraculously, after the Second World War, there appeared a new generation of excellent teachers and singers, many of them in Great Britain (which the Germans of my Berlin days had derisively named "*Das Land ohne Musík*"). Today, 1980, certain earlier works—for many years abandoned because there were no singers to sing them—[are] beautifully sung to increasingly large and delighted audiences, throughout the Western World. The explanations of this rediscovery of the art of voice training, which has made possible the revival of much unfamiliar, beautiful music, in addition to the even more difficult music by contemporary composers, are no doubt numerous. To me, they are also mysterious.

Lilli Lehmann gave one concert during that season, to which I went, of course. I was again much impressed by her stunning presence, her perfection of tone and the beauty of her *bel canto,* particularly since she was a dramatic, not a light, soprano. However, the Cavatina of the big air from Norma, a rôle in which she had long been famous, proved to be too taxing for her sixty and some years, and I was sorry that she had not foreseen this difficulty and chosen a less arduous aria. For Lehmann, as for many other great singers of her time and earlier, it is sad to know that there exists no record of their art other than that of the written word left by those who had the privilege of hearing them.

◆ ◆ ◆

I went to many other excellent concerts in Berlin that year. There were none so beautiful, however, as those of Elena Gerhardt, in a series of lieder evenings, with her close friend, the conductor, Arthur Nikisch at the piano. It is hard to describe Gerhardt's magic: voice, presence, warmth, poetic sensibility—she had them all, and today still, to have heard those two artists together remains one of my privileged experiences.

What else? The Berlin opera, of course, but here I have retained no outstanding impressions. My years in New York had probably spoilt me, for at that time the Metropolitan could and did attract the best singers from many countries. Indeed, few native American singers were to be heard there.

The Berlin theatre, on the other hand, was exciting, although for a while, my shaky German left me with an imperfect understanding of what I had seen and heard. This was particularly true of the cabaret performances, for which Berlin was famous. These were usually political sketches, very sharp and very witty, I was told, and the audiences laughed heartily.

The highlights of that season were, for me, Max Reinhardt's spectacular staging of Das Mirakel, by and this same director's revival of Frank Wedekind's long overdue, because much-censored, Frühlingserwachen.

This latter daringly frank attack—a brilliant example of early expressionism, not naturalism, as some would have it—on the criminal hypocrisy of Prussian pedagogy, although it dated from 1891, had already been a source of scandal before it finally opened under Reinhardt's direction in 1906. There had followed numerous police closures accompanied by mutilating censorship, and the play was definitively banned in 1908. Small wonder, then, that in late 1913, there should have been excitement among Wedekind's many admirers at the prospect of seeing the play as it was written, with all the censored passages restored.

But prurience dies hard. As late as 1917, during a single matinée performance on Broadway, the New York police intervened. And in 1963(!), in London, permission was grudgingly granted to stage two Sunday night performances. After two years of negotiations with the Lord Chamberlain, the play was licensed for public performance, provided that "there was no kissing, embracing or caressing between the two boys in the vineyard scene, that the words penis and vagina were omitted, and an alternative was found to the masturbation game in the reformatory."[35]

When, much later, I learned that Wedekind's parents had emigrated to the United States after the events of 1848; that they had lived for fifteen years in California and called their son Frank (not Frantz) after Benjamin Franklin, I understood why, for me, Wedekind's Expressionism was so much more human, more compassionate than that, shall we say, of Carl Sternheim.[36]

❖ ❖ ❖

35. From the foreword to the English translation by Tom Osborne, Calder & Boyars, Publishers, London, 1969.

36. See translation of Sternheim's Die Hose (in English), A Pair of Drawers, in transition VI, VII, VIII, IX, Paris, 1927.

With the arrival of Spring, I began to make plans to leave early in June, spend the summer in America and return to Berlin in September.

A happy memory of those first warm days is the picnics we organized on the café terraces that ringed the nearby Wannsee, the charm of which was enhanced at that season by the spectacle of many surrounding apple-orchards in full bloom; this, in fact, was the main attraction of the season: *das Blühen,* the flowering trees, whose feathery white reflected on the shore the white sails on the lake. I remember that I wrote my father about these excursions to feast our eyes on the *Blühen;* of how we would sit for hours on the terraces drinking coffee and munching *Kaffee Kuchen,* basking in a sense of well-being along with other singing, laughing groups like ourselves, intoxicated by the heady Spring. Father replied in a charming letter: he had often read and heard it said that Germans were apt to be a rough, insensitive people, but for him, any people who took simple pleasure in just sitting beside a lake looking at apple-trees in bloom, must be a good people.

That was mid-Spring, 1914. The Wannsee was a lovely haze of innocent white *Blühen und Segel.* But before these trees could bloom again, the Kaiser had launched his armies against his neighbours, a gesture that was to inaugurate a long period of bloody conflict and suffering in Europe. Very soon, too, the Kaiser himself, along with his pretentious dynasty, was to be swept from history for all time. To anticipate a quarter of a century later, as those terrible years advanced towards their climax, these same apple-trees, their buds still winter-bound, were to constitute the stark background against which was plotted one of the most heinous crimes in history: the Nazi government's decision to physically exterminate all Europeans of Jewish origin. The historical document that marks that event is entitled simply: "Secret Business of the Reich; minutes of the Conference held on January 20, 1942, at Berlin am Grossen Wannsee 56/58. . . ." Today this meeting, which is known as the "Wannsee Conference," is a reference that, because of what followed, strikes chill to the heart.

For neither the clear waters of the lake nor the innocence of the apple blossoms can ever again entirely efface the actions of the evil men who gathered there that day for the "working lunch" that Heydrich's invitation proposed, and during which they elaborated the plans that were to implement Hitler's criminal order.

Present were fifteen representatives, at the highest echelon, of as many ministerial and other governmental offices. Thirty copies of the day's proceedings were distributed.[37] The most elementary logistics that these figures suggest, if we

---

37. See R. Hilberg, <u>The Destruction of the European Jews</u>. London, Allen, 1961.

add to them that of the manpower numbers required to exterminate human millions, inevitably breeds scepticism as regards the supposed unawareness of these events on the part of the rest of the German population. For we know that secrets of this magnitude and this horror are inevitably leaked, if only in whispers.

Do Germans know today what was done in their name? Do their children know? It was no ordinary crime.

❖ ❖ ❖

I returned to America as planned in June (1914!). I did not, needless to say, return to Berlin in September. I was, in fact, convinced that I would never return there that I [would] spent the next five years in the United States, for the most part, in New York. But that is another story.

Actually, I did return to Berlin as the wife of Eugene Jolas in 1931, when we came to know personally some of the men—among them Gottfried Benn, Carl Sternheim, Alfred Doeblin—who, at the time of my first visit, in 1913–1914, were playing intellectually subversive rôles which, although they failed to give the results the Expressionists had hoped to achieve at that time, may perhaps be said to have contributed importantly to the more democratic German federation that we have watched rise from the blood-stained ashes of 1945.

❖ ❖ ❖

The events of August 1914 found me again in Warm Springs. I was strangely unaware of their gravity, unwilling to believe that the people among whom I had lived so recently and so pleasantly, could be as black as they were being painted.

The summer over, back in Louisville, Henry Watterson, editor of the local Courier Journal, had announced his war slogan: "To hell with the Hohenzollerns and the Hapsburgs!" Meanwhile, there soon began to arrive regularly from the Wilhelmstrasse to my Louisville address, sheafs of English-language propaganda, that only ceased coming in 1917, when America entered the war.

This latter event brought many changes, not only into the life of the nation, but also into that of the average citizen. In my family, father became a "minute man" speaker in favour of the National War Loan, mother presided a state-wide women's organization working for the same cause, both of my brothers joined the army—only Angus was sent overseas—and Cornelia's just-married husband, Kenneth Davis, joined the aviation corps. I myself took a "job" in the Louisville office of the Western Union, which involved learning the Morse code and teaching it to others. Meanwhile, a cultural boycott quickly became evident: German and Austrian performers—I recall with sorrow the affront to the gentle Fritz

Kreisler—were all denounced. Wagner's operas became anathema. Even the commercial firms that had the word "German" in their title, quickly replaced it by the patriotic term "liberty." All this in a city (Louisville) that, for many years, had been the home of a prosperous, 8-page German-language newspaper, and owed most of its musical activities to the descendants of its originally welcome German colony. It was a culturally bleak moment in the United States; my political confusion was great.

Western Europe became "over there," a place of blood and mud, where our "doughboys" spent weeks that could drag on into months "in the trenches," or occasionally went victoriously "over the top." (It is my impression that this vocabulary did not survive that war). Very early, a large army camp for some 25,000 men, Camp Zachary Taylor, was established within a street-car ride of downtown Louisville. I did what I could, either by going myself with my guitar, or rounding up others who sang, danced or what have you, for entertainment. The disoriented, bewildered young men who crowded into the Y.M.C.A. "huts" for those "do it yourself" programmes usually responded noisily to these incursions, and I have not forgotten the poor kid from the Kentucky mountain area, who thought that Camp Taylor was "over there," that he had already arrived in France.

But although this was a full and instructive year, I soon realized that my singing was getting nowhere, and when I heard of the arrival in New York from Paris of a highly recommended singing teacher, the aging Giulia Valda, herself a former opera-singer and pupil of the great Francesco Lamperti, I decided to go to New York to work with her. My mother opposed this decision, my father did not, so I went. To emphasize my desire for independence, I took a "full-time job" in the publishing-house of Charles Scribner and Sons, where my task consisted in dunning bad debtors, a very lowly feature of this big publishing house's many activities. But these were my first earnings and this fact, in addition to the absorbingly interesting singing lessons, were sources of growing confidence.

When I decided to leave Ch. Scribner and his bad debtors to solve their differences without me, I took another much more highly-coloured job, with the New York Western Union Telegraph Co. This involved learning *perfectly* two techniques: a) touch-typing—I spent a solid month of 8–hour days with my hands on hidden keys, methodically exercising each finger to be responsible for a certain number of allotted letters—and b) transmission of telegrams by telephone, which is far more subtle and more strictly codified than meets the ear. A is for Adam, and only for Adam, neither Anatole nor Annie can be substituted; F and S must never be spoken without the identifying addition of "for frank" and "for sugar." As for B, C, E, G, P, V, Z, etc.—not one of them could be left without its identifying twin, strictly the same. To have learned these things 65 years ago has stood me in as good stead as anything I ever learned. I have typed hundreds of thousands of words, and I find that I have a distinct advantage over most French telephoners because I know and understand that A is for Anatole, in France, and B for Berthe, and that these aids are essential when dictating a telegram, or even just leaving my name.

In spite of the tragedy that those war years represented for millions of Europeans, for me they were the essential ones during which the confining chrysalis of family and milieu ceased either to prejudice or favour my choices and decisions. I was working, earning, learning. I was even belatedly being made love to; a brief, searing experience to which death wrote the final word.

When the war ended and Valda returned to France, with my always indulgent father's help and blessing, I followed her, in late September 1919.

I was now 26 years old, finally an adult, with few scars that would not eventually heal, and an immense store of energy and zest, as I began the new life in Paris.

Paris, September 1919.

Just as when I had left for Berlin in 1913, living arrangements in France had kindly been made for me in advance by the Paris friend who introduced me to Giulia Valda. So it was with a precise address in hand that I arrived at the Gare St. Lazare, from where, chaperoned by this friend, I taxied to the Villa-des-Ternes, in the 17th Arrondissement of Paris. Dusk was falling as we drove through the gate; I can still feel the soft Paris air, unlike any I had experienced elsewhere, or so it seemed to me.

The Villa-des-Ternes is one of those hidden, intimate spots for which Paris planners have always seemed to possess the secret, and which live lives of their own amidst gardens and trees behind apparently quite ordinary, at times even forbidding, street-fronts. This one winds its drowsy way from No. 96 Avenue des Ternes, where it discreetly starts, to No. 27 Rue Guersant, where it as discreetly ends; the twenty or so individual houses and gardens that line both sides of its single ivy-fenced road, could be found in almost any 19th Century French suburb.

In 1919 vestiges of fortifications dating from the 1870 war were still standing beyond the nearby Porte des Ternes, which gave onto the independent community of Neuilly-sur-Seine. Further south, at the Porte Maillot, tall wrought-iron gates manned by uniformed customs inspectors, protected Neuilly's tradespeople from Parisian competition.

Much of this today bewildering neighbourhood of looped tunnels and motorways was at that time an amusement area. On the north-west corner of the Place de la Porte Maillot was "Luna Park," its *montagnes russes,* ferris-wheels and sideshows guarded by the large bronze Ballon d'Alsace that marked the entrance.

"Luna Park" provided added fun for the pleasure-loving clientèle of the popular "Foire de Neu-neu" that for several weeks each year, occupied much of
Neuilly's main avenue.

On the south-east corner of the Place de la Porte Maillot, at the entrance to
the Bois de Boulogne, stood a life-sized, topless, four-seated stone automobile—
a very early model—complete with dust-coated, goggled chauffeur and two
lady passengers in floppy hats tied under their chins with *point d'esprit* veils. I
repeat: all carved in stone! Much to my regret, after World War II, this unique
monument to modern invention had been removed. And who, today, remem-
bers "Luna Park"?

◆ ◆ ◆

The "Villa-des-Ternes" has known several metamorphoses. Originally, part of
the park surrounding the Château des Ternes, under the Restoration, it became
a public garden with what are called "attractions," consisting probably of a merry-
go-round, swings and other such innocent diversions. I learn that its single carriage road was laid out in 1822 and that by the end of the century, the former
amusement-park had given way to the lovely, green, all but secret, residence area
that it has remained.

Madame Langlois's *pension de famille,* which was to be my first Paris address—
there have been many others since!—occupied the last house on the left, beside
the Rue Guersant gate. It had been the "folly" of a late 19th Century financier
named Humbolt (there were large "H's" in several rather garish stained-glass
windows) whose not always crystal clear dealings, I was told, had forced him to
abandon the house to creditors. In 1919, my impression was that of a barely furnished, make-do gamble on the part of this courageous but impractical old
French woman who had rented it in the hope of filling it with "paying guests."
Alas!

However, I was so happy to be in Paris, to be taking in once more a new city
and a new language, that its bareness and the need to buy an oil-burning stove
and fetch the oil myself, in order to keep warm and have warm water to wash
in, did not seem a hardship. I succeeded in renting a piano, and Valda lived on
the Avenue Niel, hardly five minutes away. *La vie était belle!*

◆ ◆ ◆

Today still, the members of that curiously assorted household are indelibly en-
graved among my first recollections of life with French people. The cast of characters consisted of black-clad, gold ear-ringed Madame Langlois—a perfect
Daumier—her two grown daughters, and a witty, *bon-vivant* "gentleman friend"
of Madame's age, which I estimate as having been somewhere in her middle

sixties. There was also a leftover "dough-boy" who only appeared at meal times, and although he knew no French, found French life hilariously funny. Early on, in a tone of civilized complicity, he pointed out to me in English certain strange customs of these aborigines, such as: shaking hands all round before leaving the dining-room. "You've gotta do it," he grinned, while I watched, eager to learn.

Always the first at table, *Monsieur* would enter the dining-room rubbing big hands in gourmet anticipation. "*Alors, Maman,* what have we for lunch today?" *Maman* was a delicious cook—most French women are, or were, and it was a pleasure to witness his appreciation of her talents. *Monsieur's* daughter sang minor rôles at the Opéra Comique, but although she was frequently mentioned, we never saw her.

"Madame's" two daughters, on the contrary, were quite in evidence, and they offered a striking example of the possibilities of sibling difference. The younger girl, who was studying to become a nurse, was ironic, austere, harassed. Her sister, as I have already intimated, was different; she had a different philosophy of life; she was gay, she wore pretty, expensive clothes. She was, in fact, what, at that time, was still called a *demi-mondaine,* harking back to the play by Alexander Dumas *fils:* Le demi-monde (1855).

There is a scene in this play which used to be frequently cited: At a brilliant reception to which a young man has been brought by an older one, the young man is curious: "Where are we? Who are these people?" The older man makes the following metaphorical reply: "You have seen in fruit-shops baskets of beautiful peaches, one of which you purchased and took home with you. But when you removed the top layer the peaches underneath were not as perfect, not as fresh as the others. Well, my friend, here we are among the peaches "on the bottom of the basket," an expression that was long in use to describe these off-colour members of society and their open flouting of the real *monde.*

(Translation being one of my passions, I have reflected lengthily as to what, today, might be acceptable English equivalents of the words: *monde, demi-monde, demi-mondaine,* as they were used in the France of Dumas *fils,* and even well into the XXth Century. *Le Monde,* of course, could be translated in "retro" terms, as "Society," with a capital S (see Edith Wharton). The *demi-monde,* on the other hand, presents almost insuperable difficulties as does the most famous of its characters: the *demi-mondaine,* "La Traviata" herself.

The fact is, probably, that Victorian hypocrisy never admitted the existence in its midst of such an openly identified "immoral" social institution. It consequently resorted to such expressions as "kept woman"—what was Dreiser's "Sister Carrie"?—concubine, etcetera, neither of which conveys the truth of the mutually acceptable and usually impermanent arrangement that existed between French men with money and women with none who, in an epoch that offered few alternatives, decided to pool their attributes for their mutual advantage and pleasure.

❖ ❖ ❖

I might, of course, have wondered why one Langlois sister was dowdy and lived in her mother's uncomfortable boarding-house, while the other was elegant and lived elsewhere; but somehow I did not, and when the elder sister invited me to a party *chez elle,* I accepted with pleasure.

Due to war-time restrictions, I had probably expected to find a somewhat less bleak replica—but bleak nevertheless—of Madame Langlois's meagrely furnished house. Instead, I was ushered into a small, luxuriously furnished *bonbonnière* (literally, candy-box), where a very gay, numerous company of beautiful, elegant young women and their white-gaitered, pomaded male protectors, were chatting noisily in the high, rather shrill tone that a certain class of French people are apt to adopt on formal social occasions. There was a well-provisioned buffet, and I was introduced for the first time to the treacherously heady *apéritif.* It was a curious experience to be the only outsider in this authentic scene—not staged, that is—from <u>La Traviata</u> (Act I).

❖ ❖ ❖

There was a fourth woman in the Langlois household whom I cannot easily forget; the slavey, Berthe, who was responsible for all the most menial tasks to be performed in that large eight-room house. This over-grown pale girl, who resembled a too-white leek, had spent the four war years in the cellars of Northern France, which was heavily bombed. One day, realizing that she had not appeared at lunch-time, I asked news of her and was told that she was not well. Since I knew that her room was on the top floor, I went upstairs to ask if she needed anything. I found her shivering under insufficient cover, in a state of disarray and depression that cried out for sympathy. She recovered, of course; hardship had, I suppose, inured her. But Madame Langlois did not hide her displeasure that I should have gone to her room. The servant was not my concern. In fact, she made it clear that such an "indiscretion" on my part should not be repeated.

The mistress-servant relationship between these two women, in spite of their common experience of the terrible four-year war, was a very primitive one. Berthe was a servant, therefore she was no doubt also a petty thief. After each meal, all remaining food: sugar, butter, bread, coffee, cheese, fruit . . . was locked in a wall cupboard and the key safely stored in Madame's pocket.

❖ ❖ ❖

I later moved to another pension on the nearby Rue Demours, where life was more colourful and above all, more interesting. Unlike the sparsely populated Villa-des-Ternes pension, here there were at least forty boarders, of all ages: parents and children, a number of elderly women and a few old men, all with their medicine bottles and pill-boxes, their saltless or sugarless diets, and of course their opinions on the subject of passing events.

That was the time when the famous Landru case was being unravelled in the daily press. One very witty old lady, after listening for weeks to the gruesome revelations, asked: "Do you mean to say that this man, Landru, enticed over thirty women to a remote suburban villa, cut them in pieces and burned them in a kitchen stove?" They assured her that this was what he had done.

"Why," she observed, "that's not a crime. It's a *jeu de patience* [jigsaw puzzle]." The old lady surely did not foresee that some sixty years later, Landru and his crimes would have become just that: part of a most innocent game, *i.e.:* a publicity-oriented *jeu de l'oie* [game of "snakes and ladders"], which is played on a board with 62 winding slots, in this case, each one depicting a place of historical interest in the Department of the Yvelines, near Paris.

On one of these slots we are shown Landru and his stove, above which he is holding a victim by the ankles, her head and torso supposedly, already cooking over the well-stoked flame inside the stove. It was perhaps in the nature of things that the enormity of these crimes should eventually have to be miniaturized, for public consumption, to a ludic dimension, one of many slots in a game of pursuit to be played against the bucolic background of suggested walking-tours in the forests of St. Germain, Marly and Rambouillet.

What a rarely healthy people!

❖ ❖ ❖

The vast top floor of this pension, which had probably been the servant quarter of this large, once private house, was entirely inhabited by unattached young men, come up from the provinces to try to get a foothold in the capital.

Occasionally after dinner, when the younger guests gathered aimlessly in the "salon," I would play the out-of-tune piano to try to coax them to sing or to dance, neither of which they did spontaneously. They seemed unaccustomed to singing, and the simplest dance rhythms presented serious problems. This was the generation of 1914–1918 when, I feel sure, no patriotic French person had either sung or danced.

❖ ❖ ❖

When I think back on that winter in Paris, my evening activities all seem to have been dominated by the fact that Paris was absolutely dark. There were no lights in the streets and all windows were darkened; the war was not over, the peace-treaty had not yet been signed. One of these lightless nights brought me an adventure I could well have done without.

A fellow-passenger on the *S.S. Savoie,* returning for a visit to her native land, was Madeleine Boyd, French wife of the authoritative New York book critic, Ernest Boyd. This latter fact had attracted me to her, since I had for several years followed Boyd's literary comments with interest. In addition, although she was some years my senior, Madeleine proved to be a gay, dynamic companion, and it was agreed when we separated at Le Havre, that we would meet again in Paris, which she knew well and I not at all.

The invitation was not long in coming: dinner in a night-spot with two men, one of whom she presented as an outstanding young art critic, from Brussels.

The night-spot proved to be a clandestine Hindu restaurant that offered all the familiar features: curried rice and chutney, low lights, deep cushions, turbaned service. Madeleine was particularly gay, referring several times during dinner to the surprise she had planned for us. Finally, coffee having been served, a costumed *chasseur* was sent to fetch that rare bird, a taxi, and we drove off into the night, Madeleine still chuckling over her plan for prolonging the evening.

The taxi drew up in front of a small private house, accessible up a short flight of stone steps. The darkness was total. Very soon the door opened onto a dimly-lighted entrance-hall, and a dour middle-aged woman suggested that we follow her upstairs immediately.

Although I was far from being a child, I still did not guess what might be the programme Madeleine had planned for our entertainment. The two young men, however, especially the Belgian, seemed uncomfortable but made no protest. Madeleine, on the other hand, was highly enjoying my perplexity. Finally, from snatches of the conversation that followed, I began to realize where we were: in a bordel; and that the pleasure in store had a well-known name: *voyeurism.* No, I would not go upstairs. But being incapable of finding my way in the unfamiliar dark streets and with no available transport, I could not leave alone. I would try to make the best of this tasteless practical joke, I would wait.

With undisguised impatience, "Madame" opened a door that gave onto a small room, into which I was ushered. Fellini himself might have designed the classical setting of this little bordel parlour: pink-shaded lamps, thick pink curtains and carpets, pink-flowered wallpaper, a little gilt-legged table, and finally, two gilt-legged chairs on which were seated two scantily-dressed young women, their lingerie also pink. We nodded *bonsoir.* But where would I sit? Taking stock of the furniture, I spied a small upright piano with its half-hidden stool. This offered both a place to sit and a way of breaking the embarrassing silence. I pulled out the stool, sat down and soon began to play. The two girls seemed relieved.

They even encouraged me with their smiles to keep on playing, which I did, until the *voyeurs* came downstairs. Madeleine, I think, decided that I was something of a prig, incapable of appreciating sophisticated entertainment.

Before separating, the young Belgian invited me to go with him the next day to an exhibit at the *Petit Palais,* which I did. The visit over, I remember our walking together quite properly under the chestnut trees to the bus-stop. We were discussing the paintings, "no comment" having been tacitly agreed upon as the best way to efface the events of the previous evening.

Half a century later, in Brussels, I attended a rather large and stodgy buffet luncheon, with some sixty fellow-members of an international organization, guests of the city's most prestigious museum. The distinguished greying director, who acted as our host, came towards me, smiling. "Weren't you Maria McDonald?" he asked. I looked at him closely, I had been Maria Jolas for so many years. "And you are . . . ?" "Yes," he said, "I am." We smiled a smile of recognition. We both knew when and where we had met.

It is not impossible, however, that without some such, shall we say "untoward" experience (there exist a number of other suitable adjectives) my first months in Paris would appear today to have been an all-work-no-play time, with little to recall other than a fixed routine of singing lessons practice, French lessons, practice, in unrelieved succession.

◆ ◆ ◆

The break came in the form of an invitation from Letty's brother-in-law, Will Irwin, and his wife, Inez, to join them for a drink at the Hotel Continental. For me, who thus far had hardly left my Ternes quarter, this was something of an adventure. The Irwins, both of whom were writers—Will was especially known for his very knowledgeable liberal political analyses, while Inez was a novelist—were in Paris to cover the Peace Conference, and I listened wide-eyed to his accounts of the inside negotiations taking place in Versailles.

When their party broke up, another American guest, Elsie Arden, from San Francisco, suggested that since we were going in the same direction we share a difficult-to-find taxi. As she got out, she held out her hand: "Come and see me some time, why not next Tuesday?" Needless to say, I went on Tuesday, grateful to the Irvins for having rescued me from what was doubtless a lonely routine, however absorbing the "works and days."

Elsie, who was some fifteen years my senior, was also a singer. She had that rare voice, a genuine contralto, and with the fervour that marked everything she did—enthusiasms and distastes were equally emphatic—her singing was moving and impressive. But at that time Elsie was facing the downhill side of what had evidently been a precociously begun quarter-century of personal triumphs. Not only the rare voice, but great beauty and wit, a wild zest for life, plus disregard for convention, had kept her on the crest of an apparently endless wave. This was no longer the case; the wave had crested and was beginning to break. Although the old automatisms of gaiety and "life of the party" were still evident, they were becoming more strident, more apt to be punctuated by moodiness and resentment. Thus far it had always been she who chose and dismissed the men in her life. Now she was faced with a chafing desire to be free on the part of the handsome, tall young Frenchman, Georges Duthuit, who had been sharing the comfortable flat overlooking the Place des Invalides that a fellow Californian, Noël Sullivan, had placed at her disposal.

Georges's recent stay at Oxford University, and his close association there with the esthetic teachings of the prestigious Matthew Prichard, lent added lustre to his native brilliance. He it was who introduced many well-known Parisian figures into the pleasant sixth-floor flat, who could range from Rasputin's assassin, the tall, pale Prince Youssopov, to the Russian-born sculptor Ossip Zadkine, or the painter-poet, Max Jacob, whose predictably witty comments never failed to be greeted with delight.

Needless to say, at that time, most of the rapid, subtle exchanges that took place were caviar to me, my understanding of the language being still in its early, utilitarian stages. I did understand, however, that Max Jacob's wit was the kind that stimulated wit in his listeners, and that Duthuit who, himself, had a caustic, baroque gift of expression, was never at a loss to parry his thrusts.

Jacob, who was of Jewish origin, had been converted to Roman Catholicism. His arrest by the Nazis, at well over sixty, and his resulting death, in 1944, in the Drancy detention camp, were among the more odious crimes perpetrated in the context of Nazi and Vichy anti-semitism.

❖ ❖ ❖

It was Georges, too, who organized occasional dinners in the sculptor Brancusi's studio, where we cooked beefsteaks over the coals of a large Romanian peasant stove built by the sculptor himself. Brancusi was a genial host who evidently enjoyed the rôle. The work of this very original newcomer from Eastern Europe, which combined rusticity with great elegance—all of the bronze and marble pieces were entirely refined by hand—was beginning to attract attention, particularly in the United States, where the curious swan's-neck figure entitled "Mlle-Pogany," and the beautiful golden bird poised for vertical flight, soon became familiar to all who followed these Paris events.

❖ ❖ ❖

Maria McDonald (later, Jolas) in her family home, St. James Court, in Louisville, Kentucky (seated at the bottom of the stairs with her family), 1910. Courtesy of the Beinecke Rare Book and Manuscript Library, Yale University

Eugene and Jacques Jolas, brothers, in their second year in the United States, 1911–1912. Courtesy of the Beinecke Rare Book and Manuscript Library, Yale University.

1   APRIL, 1927

transition

James Joyce, Kay Boyle, Carl Sternheim, Marcel Jouhandeau,
Hjalmar Söderberg, F. Boillot, Gertrude Stein, André Gide
Robert M. Coates, Philippe Soupault, Archibald Mac Leish,
Paul Eldridge, R. Ellsworth Larsson, Else Lasker-Schüler,
Ludwig Lewisohn, Virgil Geddes, Marcel Noll, Bravig Imbs,
Hart Crane, Evan Shipman, Georg Trakl, Robert Desnos,
Pavel Tselitsieff, Max Ernst, L. Tihanyi, Robert Sage.

Principal Agency : SHAKESPEARE and CO.
12, rue de l'Odéon, Paris, VI°

Price { 10 francs
{ 50 cents.

transition *cover no. 1, April 1927. Courtesy of the Beinecke Rare Book and Manuscript Library, Yale University.*

Eugene Jolas, Paris, 1931.
Courtesy of the Beinecke Rare
Book and Manuscript Library,
Yale University.

Portrait of Maria Jolas,
1939–1940. Courtesy of the
Beinecke Rare Book and Manu-
script Library, Yale University.

Henri Matisse drawing of Claude Duthuit, 1940. Courtesy of the Beinecke Rare Book and Manuscript Library, Yale University.

The Cantine La Marseillaise, at 789 Second Avenue (Foyer des Vétérans Français, New York), with cake in form of the sign for the Free French, 1945. Courtesy of the Beinecke Rare Book and Manuscript Library, Yale University.

Eugene Jolas reading, summer of 1951. Courtesy of the Beinecke Rare Book and Manuscript Library, Yale University.

Nathalie Sarraute and Maria Jolas in Chérence, 1960. Courtesy of the Beinecke Rare Book and Manuscript Library, Yale University.

Maria Jolas at antiwar rally (against the war in Vietnam), October 21, 1967. Courtesy of the Beinecke Rare Book and Manuscript Library, Yale University.

Maria Jolas at her desk in her Paris apartment, 106 bis rue de Rennes, in 1970. Courtesy of the Beinecke Rare Book and Manuscript Library, Yale University.

Maria Jolas walking past her former school, L'Ecole Bilingue de Neuilly, 1970. Courtesy of the Beinecke Rare Book and Manuscript Library, Yale University.

Maria Jolas with her children and grandchildren (standing: Frédéric, Claire, Gilles, Antoine, Tina; seated in front: Paule, Betsy, Maria), 1971. Courtesy of the Beinecke Rare Book and Manuscript Library, Yale University.

Pierre Vidal-Naquet, the classicist and Maria's friend, September 1975. Courtesy of the Beinecke Rare Book and Manuscript Library, Yale University.

Wyndham Lewis's drawing of James Joyce, 1920 (shown at the Joyce exhibition arranged by Maria Jolas, at the bookstore La Hune, in 1949). Courtesy of the Beinecke Rare Book

James Joyce with the painter Augustus John, late 1920s. Courtesy of the Beinecke Rare Book and Manuscript Library, Yale University.

James Joyce with Sylvia Beach and Adrienne Monnier in the bookstore Shakespeare and Co., 1920s. Courtesy of the Beinecke Rare Book and Manuscript Library, Yale University.

James Joyce and the surrealist author Philippe Soupault (published in transition*), 1930. Courtesy of the Beinecke Rare Book and Manuscript Library, Yale University.*

"Le Trio," inscription on this photograph by Lucia Joyce: James, Lucia, and Nora Joyce, 1932. Courtesy of the Beinecke Rare Book and Manuscript Library, Yale University.

Tina Jolas listening to Hilary Caws tell a story in the garden of the poet René Char. Courtesy of the Beinecke Rare Book and Manuscript Library, Yale University.

My favourite evening place, also organized by Georges, was dinner "*Chez Baty,*" corner Montparnasse and Raspail, after which we moved across the Boulevard to the Rotonde where often, until the early hours of morning, the new *esthétique,* particularly in its cubist and abstract manifestations, was hotly debated. I have not forgotten Duthuit's pessimistic comment, on one of these occasions: "If things continue like that," he said, "by the end of the century, there will be no more art." With most of the great XXth Century painters and sculptors now dead (as I write this in 1981), and a new generation yet to impose its talents, the next decades will show whether Duthuit's gloomy prediction was justified. It was his conviction, one that he has brilliantly expounded in his writings,[38] that the soil in which great art flourishes is that of an exalting faith, the rise and decline of which it inevitably espouses. If we apply this criterion to the two "faiths" that have most deeply marked our own century—Nazism and Marxist Leninism—we are obliged to conclude that, their fanatic exaltation notwithstanding, the results have been not art, but propaganda. There will remain little art inspired by either of these "faiths" other than rare poetic words of revolt against their repressive regimes.

For me, these discussions were a quite new experience. Thus far my aesthetic surroundings had been confined to music and literature. Now I was acquiring an entirely new vocabulary, words whose English equivalents I had not yet used, and which opened up for me new avenues of sensibility, accessible this time, through the eye. That in itself was exciting: learning to read what a painter or a sculptor had expressed, to recognize the artist's personality as one would a handwriting or a tone of voice. And I became convinced that in a city like Paris—does there exist another such city?—where the visual arts have flourished for so many centuries, even the most insensitive eye would eventually see forms and colours with increased awareness. It is not for nothing that Paris has been called the painter's city.

❖ ❖ ❖

But I should like to return briefly to the man, Duthuit, whose sharp intelligence and radiant personality cannot be disposed of in a few casual references.

Georges Duthuit was provincially born and bred, an orphan "raised," as we say in the South, by a peasant grandmother towards whom he vowed deep gratitude and veneration. He used to say that he had spent seven years in the army: two years of "military service," the four war years, and one more, waiting to be

---

38. Cf. <u>Représentation et Présence, Premiers Écrits et Travaux, 1923–1952</u>. Introduction by Yves Bonnefoy. Flammarion, 1974.

demobilized. It was during these years that finally he passed his *baccalauréat,* prepared as best it could be in between military *corveés.* With what help he succeeded in emerging from these confining circumstances, I cannot say. But unlike many French intellectuals, he did not pursue further academic degrees, a fact that, in France, where often brilliant specialists continue for years to seek ever higher academic honours, excluded him from an official post. It could not, however, exclude him from pursuing his own very original interests and investigations, and he remained, until his death in 1973, a scathing critic of most contemporary aesthetic theory. To André Malraux 's <u>Musée Imaginaire</u>, he replied with a two-volume rebuttal entitled: <u>Le Musée Inimaginable</u>. He saw our time as miserably deprived of the genuine richness that a less materialistic, more exigent critical taste might have provided.

His own first and most enduring aesthetic shock had been the all-embracing faith, and its expression in all the arts, of Byzantine ritual. He was, in fact, still in his twenties when he published the slender volume entitled: <u>Byzance</u>[39] that first focused informed attention on the originality and independence of his thinking.

During World War II, in New York, where Georges Duthuit was one of the U.S. Government's most effective French broadcasters against Nazi conquest and Vichy collaboration, he participated with Claude Lévi-Strauss, André Breton and Max Ernst, in locating and assembling specimens of the little-known artworks by the Indians of the Canadian Pacific coast. These were objects which in the general assessment of Indian art, had thus far remained neglected, and, in many cases, had been relegated to the junk-shops of New York.

◆ ◆ ◆

Sadly, the last ten years of Duthuit's life were those of an invalid. His personality and ideas, consequently, have remained, as it were, confidential, unknown to the general public. The handful of men and women who were his friends, however, will not soon forget the rare passion and immense cultural resources that subtended his activities.

They know too that, in spite of the frequently Baroque convolutions of his own literary style, to quote the homely "forty-niner" who, seeing the Rocky Mountains for the first time said, "There's gold in them hills," digging for Duthuit's gold can be richly rewarding. Georges Duthuit left the Rue de l'Université *appartement,* and shortly afterwards married the daughter of Henri Matisse. Elsie's resentment did not diminish with the years. She died in New York shortly after

---

39. One of the original Zurich Dadaists, Hugo Ball, also published, in 1931, a <u>Byzantinisches Christentum</u>.

World War II, still consumed by the bitterness she had been unable to dominate. She remained a kind friend to me and I have not forgotten that it was at a party she gave to introduce the young pianist, Jacques Jolas, who was soon to make his Paris debut, that I met Eugene Jolas. "I hear the brother is intelligent," Elsie said, "I think I'll invite him." He was indeed intelligent, and our courtship, which started at that party, could have been described as "whirl-wind." That was in 1925. But I am anticipating.

A few years after this marriage, I was asked by Henri Matisse to come to see him at the Hotel Lutetia, where he was stopping on one of his visits to Paris. I had no idea of what he could possibly want to talk to me about. I was a rank outsider to the upper reaches of the Art World, our only link could have been his daughter, Marguerite, who was married to my good friend, Georges Duthuit.

Marguerite, he told me, was not happy. Georges had proved to be something of a philanderer, who apparently could charm the birds—of whatever sex—out of the trees and, himself, liked to bask in the pleasure of their song. Conclusion: he would always be a philanderer, he was a poor husband, she should leave him.

But here, he added, that fateful blindness, LOVE, had raised its deceptively beautiful head. What was love? he asked impatiently. A sharp denunciatory analysis followed. I knew, of course, that Georges was attracted to women, and that usually, they were attracted to him. But I had not followed his marriage. What had happened?

Very much embarrassed by the great Matisse's revelation of his own proprietary attitude towards this frail daughter who, as she often told me later, had devoted her entire youth to him and his art, I could only suggest that such situations usually found their own solution. It was not a comfortable dialogue.

Today all three protagonists are gone. And fate so decreed that the situation did live by its own solutions for nearly a half-century longer.

◆ ◆ ◆

In the Spring of 1924, I returned to Louisville for a visit, Mother being still far from recovered from the shock and grief caused by my brother Angus' accidental death two years earlier, and which had left her nervously exhausted. She planned to return to France with me to take the cure for her persistent neuralgia at Aix-les-Bains. Our bags were packed and we were ready to leave the next day, when someone called to say that Father, who had been speaking to a business group in favour of a Good Roads Bill for the deprived mountain counties, had suffered a severe stroke and been removed to a hospital. After twenty-four hours of what, from the start, had evidently been a losing vigil, he died without gaining consciousness. As the first deep, impressive breathing gradually weakened, almost imperceptibly, we saw that this great oak of a man, who had never been ill, was dying, had died. For me, I knew that I had lost not only my Father, but also my dearest friend. "Only death could conquer such a man," was how one Louisville editorialist ended his tribute.

◆ ◆ ◆

The two month's cure at Aix-les-Bains brought some alleviation of Mother's neuralgia, she returned to Louisville as planned, in September. Callously enough, I did not return with her; I simply could not face the months of total submission to her unhappy tyranny that my return would inevitably have entailed. I was 31 years old, my share of Father's estate amply covered my needs, a fact that Mother resented. In her view, I should not have been given complete independence, my purse-strings should have been left in her hands. After all, I was not married—the three others were—which fact lowered my status to that of a minor. Exactly when, according to that creed, an unmarried woman ceased to be a minor to become an "old-maid," would be hard to say. But once the label was hung around her neck, there was little chance of reprieve: she could, of course, become a secretary or a school teacher. Nor did either of these activities preclude devoting the rest of her life to her parents, frequently, her salary as well. This bleak code of conduct between the generations did not, I believe, survive the second World War. It remains to be seen whether the segregation of old from young that has replaced it, that is, homes for the widowed, and geriatric communities for couples, will give satisfaction. Live and let live, yes, only not *together.*

This is a new concept, more honest too, perhaps, than the old one of traditionally imposed harmony. Only here the forgotten ingredient, even when all material problems are eliminated, is the sense of isolation and exclusion that can accompany the process of aging and the inexorable approach of extinction. The key words to make this harsh reality tolerable are perhaps mutual forbearance and empathy. But words can do only so much, the rest must come from the heart and from recognition of a mutual debt.

◆ ◆ ◆

With this difficult but essential decision behind me, my life seemed to offer new perspectives. I have described the party at which I met Eugene Jolas, and this leads me to a moment of self-analysis.

Already, as a girl, I had sensed that I did not attract, nor was I attracted by the young men I knew, other than as members of a group. Sing or dance with them, yes, but no hand-holding, or "goo-goo eyes," as the song went, with any of them. Psychoanalysts would probably find a "pat" explanation of this fact in my love for my father, or some latent lesbian instinct. Let them prate! Ours was an extremely decorous, formal family life. There were no whiffs of sex in the air, let alone incestuous whiffs, that could have been detected by even the most sophisticated nose. As for lesbianism, I didn't know the word until I came to France in 1919. Nor am I unaware of what is said to take place in the unconscious. But here, it seems to me, each one of us should know best what is locked in that cellar-room. Mine was locked and *empty,* until I had passed my 22nd birthday. And I am inclined to think that this mutual lack of attraction, in addition to what is quaintly described as "late flowering," was also due to my desire for independent action and thought, which may well have frightened off most of the young men of my generation. To share the blame, I shall add, however, that there were no geniuses among them either, who might have startled me into recognition of the importance of the man-woman relationship. In Eugene Jolas I had met a men whose mind and heart I immediately respected and loved. He had the strengths I lacked, and my strengths complemented his. I knew, too, that life being the fortuitous affair that it is—"a tale told by an idiot"—this felicitous meeting might also never have taken place, that fate was on my side.

❖ ❖ ❖

As 1925 advanced, and our need for each other increased, an unexpected event supplied the answer to what was becoming the question I knew I must soon ask myself in total honesty: was I still as determined as I had been to pursue a professional singing career?

The reply came as a shock, but it was nevertheless a reply. Giulia Valda died suddenly and unpredictably, of heart failure, as it was then called. At this news, instinctively I realized that although I would always sing, it would not be professionally. I would fit my life to Gene's.

❖ ❖ ❖

As the Spring, then Summer of 1925 advanced, our intention to make our lives together became more precise: we would get married. In the late Autumn, I left for America to tell my mother this news, and a few weeks later, Gene followed. As our plans materialized, Gene said timidly: "On my Mother's account I should like to be married in Church," to which I of course assented, really I didn't care. But my own Mother, when she realized that because I was not a Catholic, I would be married in a back parlour, on the Madison Avenue side of St. Patrick's Cathedral, was privately indignant. Good soldier that she was, however, she nevertheless signed her name as witness and refrained from telling either Gene or the priest who officiated, what she thought of Catholic intolerance. For myself,

Catholics were "like that," and light-heartedly, I signed a paper to the effect that our children would be brought up in the Catholic faith. Of this, more anon. My intentions were honest, but I did not succeed.

◆ ◆ ◆

Chapter V

Gene, who knew the newspaper "ropes," soon uncovered a job on a New Orleans newspaper—The ITEM TRIBUNE and after a fortnight spent in seeing old friends and places in New York—Gene was sentimentally attached to places—he left, filled with optimism for the new city, the very name of which echoed romantically in the French lobes (as opposed to the German ones) of his Lorraine-bred brain.

Although we only lived six months in New Orleans, I have retained a happy, sun-drenched memory of that interlude in our life together. One of these memories has to do with my arrival in the city, where Gene had preceded me, I having stopped off for a few days in Louisville on my way south.

I found Gene lodged in a former colonial "mansion" that had been converted into what was evidently a discreet, private house of, shall we say, convenience. Gene, who seemed unaware of this metamorphosis (I feel sure that his taxi-driver had been well aware of it, however), had rented a large double room in which, on a centre table, in a glass vase, he had put, to welcome me, one beautiful pink rose. If there had been a dozen roses, I could not have been more touched. Gene was still something of a social bear in those days, and his pockets were certainly not full. Whatever storms were to mark our quarter-century of life together— they were not many, really, we made a good team—that New Orleans rose remained for me the symbol of the "tie that binds."

We soon found a little furnished house with back garden, on St. Peter Street, in the heart of the French quarter, from where we could hear the calliopes— how their strange music fascinated Gene!—on the pleasure-boats in the harbour.

In addition to the city itself, with its lazy charm and many historical associations, there were a number of writers there that winter, either passing through, or settled for a few months in view of a book to be written. This was the case with Sherwood Anderson,[40] who was living there with his third and very charming wife, Elizabeth, and a son by his first wife, who worked on the same paper that Gene did.[41]

---

40. The book was Black Laughter.
41. I shall return to this trio later.

There was too, a brief visit from Edmund Wilson, whose dynamic intelligence we greatly enjoyed. Wilson joined us for a trip up the *Bayou Tèche* in a rented Ford, with me at the wheel. We were invited to stay overnight by a "gentleman farmer," Weeks Hall, who had occasionally found his way to Paris, where I had known him, but whose permanent home was on the bank of the Tèche, where he lived in a vast, white-pillared house with tall camellia trees blooming in the front garden.

Weeks trotted out for our benefit all the most spectacular features of the native folk-lore, including a mysterious, unidentified—neither guest nor servant—dark-skinned beauty, who set Wilson to wondering. (Ah! these Southern gentlemen!) He also served us a delicious *café brûlot,* which he brewed with all the required spices, in a large copper recipient that had nothing to fear from the flaming brandy that floated on the surface of the coffee.

Among the native *literati,* the group around the excellent "little" magazine: The Double Dealer,[42] were warmly hospitable. They were on the point of folding, and for a brief moment, Gene, who had a bee in his bonnet about starting a literary magazine, was tempted to take over the Double Dealer. However, fate decreed differently, and an amusing fate it was.

We were already in the month of May, the weather was hot and oppressive, when one day Gene was assigned to cover a Shriners' luncheon. In anticipation of possible boring moments, he had taken with him a book by André Gide for diversion. I recall that at that time, practically all French books, belonging in whatever category, were similarly bound in lemon-yellow paper. Gene was among the first to leave the dining-room.

On his way to the exit he was accosted by one of the Shriners: "What's that book you got there?" On his guard, Gene replied, "It's a book I'm reading." Infuriated, the Shriner, who had noticed the unfamiliar yellow binding, retorted: "It ain't American, is it?" "No," said Gene, "it's French." "Well, you know,"—the man was becoming threatening—"around here we're all Americans, and we don't want no foreigners here."

Gene did not answer. But that evening, when he arrived home he announced firmly, "We're leaving!" And leave we did, as soon as our tenuous hold on life in that beautiful city could be liquidated. Not without regrets, however, and to efface the memory of the Shriner's intolerance, I like to recall that it was in the Cathedral at New Orleans that I first saw white and black people kneeling together in Holy worship. That, too, was Catholicism.

As our preparations for leaving advanced, my regrets diminished, for I realized that the child I was carrying would need a more permanent home than that

42. 1922–1926

afforded by our superficially-rooted implantation in this, to us, lovely, but unfamiliar city.

We said good-bye with genuine affection to the Andersons and other new friends, with promises to write and not forget. The New Orleans summer was already almost intolerably hot when we left in June for New York, from where we sailed immediately.

❖ ❖ ❖

Chapter VI

Paris again . . . how happy we were to be back! In no time we had found a comfortable, furnished flat just off the Place de Breteuil, behind the Invalides, and in a few weeks, Gene had found a job on the Paris edition of the <u>Chicago Tribune</u>. We were now ready to give the expected heir or heiress a warm welcome.

It turned out to be an heiress, Betsy, and I have many happy memories of her arrival on a soft August evening, in a Passy nursing-home. My room gave on to tree-shaded gardens and friendly, open windows, through one of which a woman's voice could be heard singing her baby to sleep: "*Le Marchand de sable*" (Sandman), she sang, had passed by and had left sand in baby's eye. The day had come to a happy close, now it was time to *faire dodo* (go sleepy-bye). Every evening she sang this song, which I soon came to know by heart, and later, for many years, sang to my own children and grandchildren. I have never heard it since, but it became part of my nursery repertoire, still bathed in soft twilight air and the happiness at holding my own baby in my arms.

There was one jarring note during that fortnight, which I have not forgotten. Gene had a good friend in the French poet, Paul Eluard. It was an accepted custom for wives to call on the mother and new-born child of friends. One day, therefore, Mme Gala Eluard knocked on the door of my sick-room.

After a few words of introduction—I had never met her—she approached the baby in its crib. "*Quelle horreur!*" was her only comment. Was this merely a surrealist pose? Possibly. She did not stay long married to the gentle Eluard, and later became the wife of Salvador Dali. Our paths never crossed again.

❖ ❖ ❖

When I first met Gene, he had been living for several years in small Left Bank hotels, a situation that had precluded all hospitality beyond that of a shared café table. Now he could invite friends to his home, and we very soon did do a lot of casual inviting. The young poet Bravig Imbs came with his violin to play violin duets with Gene, to my accompaniment, and there was even a large, impromptu cocktail party that, but for Gene's alertness, could have become the scene of a "diplomatic incident" between two important members of the ruling surrealist "junta," one of whom, Philippe Soupault, had, that very morning, been expelled from the group for suspected "leaks." The other important surrealist expected was Paul Eluard. A meeting on that day of these two, no matter on how neutral an occasion, Gene felt, should be avoided, if possible.

So Soupault, who was first to arrive, was immediately closeted behind shut doors, while my role was to watch for Eluard's arrival, introduce him into the salon with the other guests, *close the door* to the salon, and once the coast was clear, release the suspect from his hiding-place and escort him to the front door. The scenario was carried out to the letter. Although Soupault was, I believe, the first surrealist to be expelled, he is, as I write, the last surviving member, except Louis Aragon, of the original founding group. But before leaving that cocktail-party, I recall that it was also the occasion of my first and only meeting with Ernest Hemingway.

The party was at its height, standing-room only, and much noisy talk. I had not heard the kitchen door-bell, when the cleaning woman knocked to say that a man there had asked to speak to me. I was greeted by a tall, smiling young man wearing a blue overall, which was the typical French worker's uniform, but I knew, too, that it had also been adopted by certain well-known painters to protect their street clothes.

"Excuse me, Mrs. Jolas," said the smiling young man on the kitchen landing, "I'm Ernest Hemingway. Gene invited me to your party. But when your concierge saw my blue overall, she refused to let me come up the front stairs." The concierge, no doubt, was doing her job, as she understood it. I am not so sure about the motives of our guest. After all, he was a writer, not a painter, and the date was not *Mardi Gras.*

◆ ◆ ◆

In addition to such motley company as came to that cocktail-party, there was a group of close musical friends around Jacques Jolas, with whom Gene and I immediately fraternized as though we had always known them. These were: Jean and Ysa d'Elbée, Rosalie Campbell, a witty, aging maiden lady who, although she was British, was somehow related to the entire Faubourg St. Germain; and last but far from least, an imperturbable, massive Dane, Paul Rosenstand, whose chief concern was that one day he should be awakened before noon by loud knocking on the door of his hotel room and a peremptory voice demanding: "*Vos papiers!,*" of which, of course, he had none.

Jean d'Elbée was an authentic marquis, a direct descendant of the royalist general who was shot during the war of the Chouans, and himself a debonair, witty intellectual, whose meagre earnings (or so I gathered) were derived from an editorial position on the staff of the by that time all but clandestine <u>Revue de Paris</u>. His Spanish wife, Ysa, was an excellent pianist, as well as the light-hearted mother of six young d'Elbées. As for the Dane, in addition to his gift for solemn fun, he was a monument of musical erudition.

Together they introduced me to a new Bohemia: the European aristocratic poor. I was familiar with their Virginia counterparts. But that is not quite an accurate comparison, either, for the events that had made these people poor lay so far behind them that there remained little trace of an actual impact. What they had miraculously retained, however, was an ease of manner, a sense of play and, above all, an amenity and excellence of speech that were a pleasure to the ear. A common bond, no doubt, was that they were all equally impecunious.

As I recall these friends of 1926, so long ago, I marvel that they engaged in no political discussions that I can remember. For them, there seemed to exist neither "left" nor "right," and today I can but wonder at this fact, after witnessing the bitter political divisions that have characterized French life since World War II. An old American resident in Paris put it wittily in a recent talk he gave to a group of American business-men. To the question: "Do the French like us?" He replied, "They don't like each other, why should they like us?"

A Dutch philosopher is quoted as having said that "there is no wound which time cannot heal." In our century, we have seen the deepest of West European wounds: Franco-German rivalry, after terrible blood-lettings, finally healed through the will and prayers of two old men, Charles de Gaulle and Konrad Adenauer, who determined that their two peoples should live in peace. And thus far, time would appear to have favoured their determination.

But beyond Europe, there remain stubborn, dangerous antagonisms. The aggressive, frequently mendacious vocabulary of their hatred must be drowned by the sound of other words expressing other hopes. As we approach the new millennium, with its unprecedented promise of a more livable life for greater numbers, we shall have to "cast out the old Adam" and force ourselves to *imagine* and *experiment* with other, fairer ways of living together.

In my generation, it is a truism to say that time and distance have been reduced to minimum requirements. Also, little by little, the "age of contempt" is giving way to an "age of concern," and this in itself is a promise. But we shall need more than two old men to make the peace the world so sorely needs today. For evil and greed are permanent realities and there are both young and old men —powerful ones—who for the third time in this century, cast an ominous shadow on what could be a sunny world. They do not want to live in peace.

❖ ❖ ❖

Chapter VII

Meanwhile, Betsy was prospering, a calm, happy baby, and Gene's thoughts were evolving every day more precisely towards the magazine he hoped to publish. The situation was not, however, as simple as it had seemed.

In the South of France, the very talented young Irish-American, Ernest Walsh, with a Scots friend, Ethel Moorhead, had brought out three interesting issues of This Quarter. I recall that Gene sent them a manuscript entitled: By Radio To God. Walsh wrote him a cordial, friendly letter in which he pointed out that "God was a very big word." Gene did not doubt this for a moment; he had used this "very big word" for that reason, in fact, his faith having become once more, after ten years of virulent agnosticism, unshakable, which it remained until the end. I don't remember whether or not Walsh, who died in 1926, before This Quarter No. 3, appeared, published Gene's poems. Those were Godless times. His death was deeply felt by all who had known him. He left a posthumous daughter[43] whose mother is Kay Boyle. Ernest Walsh will not be forgotten.

In addition to the existence of This Quarter, Ezra Pound had brought out four issues of a new magazine entitled The Exile (Spring '27–Fall '28). He said afterwards, however, that had he known of transition's plans, he would not have done so.

Actually, Gene envisaged a more far-ranging type of magazine than either of these two, which were devoted principally to English and United States writing. Gene's organically acquired familiarity with both French and German literatures —I recall his German mother and French father, his first schooling in the German-language schools of Lorraine followed by two years in French-speaking Metz, then his ten years' experience of American journalism. These combined to set his sights beyond presentation of only American and English writers. He was painfully aware of the "malady of language." He sensed, too, that there was a spirit of experimentation abroad in all the arts, and he wanted to give expression to the experimenters, wherever they were: build bridges between them through translations, informed criticism, and, for the plastic arts, good photographic reproductions. He decided to consult Sylvia Beach who, after her publication of Ulysses, with her friend Adrienne Monnier, had made of Nos. 7 and 12 Rue de l'Odéon, essential points of contact for writers in Paris.

Sylvia proved to be most encouraging: "I believe that Joyce would be interested in your project; he is looking for a non-commercial publisher for serial

43. Sharon, today Mrs. John Cowling, who lives in Paris as do her three children and two grand-children.

publication of his new work, a publisher with whom he can consult in close, regular contact. Go and see him."

Gene was already somewhat familiar with the new work through a few fragments that had appeared here and there.[44] He was aware of the immensity of the technical problems involved. But undaunted, he went to see Joyce. He returned elated by the promise of Joyce's collaboration, and charmed by the cordiality with which Joyce had received him.

◆ ◆ ◆

Then came the practical considerations: he would need editorial and secretarial assistance. Where would he find them? I seemed to be the obvious choice for secretary; but the co-editor? That presented more of a problem, since there were several essential requirements to be met: a) he would have to be either an Englishman or an American; b) he would have to write acceptable literary English, know the techniques of copy, preparation and proof-reading. In addition, he should be a judge of good writing. The choice fell upon Elliot Paul, a colleague of Gene's at the Paris <u>Chicago Tribune</u>, with whom he had had many congenial literary discussions. Paul had also published three well received novels in America. So Paul was approached. He enthusiastically accepted.

And what an attractive, elusive creature he was! Ready laughter and ready wit, quick with quip and judgement, his presence added zest to any gathering. He was also, at first, a diligent co-editor. His influence was more grass-roots American than Gene's, as well as his awareness of what he saw as the still dominating influence of puritanism on American intellectual life, with its resulting parochialism. These were mentalities that he felt <u>transition</u> should mercilessly combat. After all, Paul was a New Englander, from the Boston area. It is not impossible that his own libertarian ideas and life-style had already, at that time, come in for criticism.

Gene, on the other hand, now that the harshness of his early American years lay far behind him, had become fervently imbued with the American "way." But paradoxically, he had also remained essentially the product (at times, rebellious) of Lorraine Catholicism and, more especially, of German Romanticism. The XXth Century European manifestations of earlier currents: *i.e.,* Expressionism, Dada and Surrealism, interested him profoundly; however altered, their sources were still recognizable. Conversely, he was indifferent to certain agnostic, materialistic thinking that also characterized his time.

---

44. For an excellent account of the literary background against which <u>transition</u> first appeared see: <u>transition: The History of a Literary Era 1927–38</u> by Dougald McMillan, Calder and Boyars, Ltd., London, 1975. A United States edition of this book was published by George Braziller at the same time.

His hopes for <u>transition</u> were, among others, to make known the best features of these modern movements. At the same time it should lead to a sharpening of the artist's instrument, and an expanding awareness of hitherto undreamed-of potentialities for spiritual renewal. In other words, his was a subjective, aesthetic vision, rather than one of social reform. Geographically he hoped to bridge the Atlantic ocean, to include the talents of the entire western hemisphere. In fact, the name "Bridge" had been seriously considered before it was abandoned for the title of Edwin Muir's recently published volume of essays, <u>Transition</u> (1926).

A few years later, when the fascinated gaze of many of his contemporaries was still fixed on the events of 1917 and the emergence of Soviet Russia, in a much decried article entitled <u>Super-Occident</u> (<u>transition</u> No. 15, 1929), Gene expressed his conviction concerning the continuing pre-eminence of the Occident in world affairs. He had never travelled east of Czechoslovakia. But honesty compels me to say that since his death in 1952, I have seen few developments in those regions that would have caused him to change his viewpoint.

Muir's insistence on the importance for the critic to deal with "things of the present . . ." as well as with the "tendencies which have not yet found a decisive direction," was a particularly felicitous formulation that corresponded to Gene's vision. With Muir's permission, the name <u>transition</u> was agreed upon. Today I am impressed by its aptness, not only as regards the epoch of 1927–1938, but also this entire century, which one feels, is still in the throes of a painful, inevitable transition. Towards what? To quote my good friend the historian, Arno Mayer, "No one has a clue."

In 1928, Gene wrote, "It is so end-of-world in me," and there is still no lack of doomsday apprehension. Meanwhile, the glaring defects of today's world are so universally condemned that, in all probability, humanity can and will win this combat of its own making, and begin again, more humbly, more generously, along less dangerous lines. "World without end" was not an idle formulation. Why abandon it out of arrogant rivalry when there's room for us all?

It is possible that Elliot Paul was more or less indifferent to Gene's objectives, I couldn't say. He and I usually met over questions of copy preparation, or proofreading, and I could always laugh at the drollery of his comments on French life, which were still those of a fresh impact on a witty American awareness. We arranged to give him a sufficient salary to allow him to work shorter hours at the "Trib," and soon gestation of <u>transition</u> No. 1 was well under way, leaving just enough space on the dining-room table for meals, which were now confined to one side, since <u>transition</u> occupied the other three. A printer had been found in Mayenne (the same one who had printed <u>Ulysses</u>); possible copy was being read, retained or rejected, translated, re-typed, made clear to French printers, etc. There was, in fact, "never a dull moment," and I soon realized that I would need every ounce of my maniacal insistence on material order to remain on top of the paper chaos that these two men were able to create in a few hours.

It was about at this moment—January 1927, shall we say—that Charles Boni, of the New York publishing firm *Boni and Liveright*, passed through Paris and called to see us. The rumour had reached New York that there was a new magazine in the offing; he was curious. We showed him our table of contents for the first number, he was impressed. "Why," he said, "you've got there a commercial gold-mine." He could not believe that we did not intend to exploit it. But we clung to our principle, which had been accepted by all of our contributors: 20 francs a page to all alike and the authors retained the copyright. Quite evidently, too, any departure from that arrangement would not only have been a source of infinite complications, but would also have completely altered the nature of Gene's undertaking. It is interesting to recall that certain contributors did not accept payment, and others, for instance, Harry Crosby and James Sweeney, kindly helped to settle the bills when our own funds were low.

◆ ◆ ◆

It was [around] this time that Gene began to say that he could not live in Paris any longer. "Too many people," he moaned. "I can't think, I'll go out of my mind." So, attentive wife that I was, I went to a real-estate agent on the rue Castiglione to ask what he had to propose in the way of a quiet furnished country-place for rent by the year, "neither too far from, nor too near Paris; neither too uncomfortable, nor too expensive, etc."

He did not appear at all dismayed by my stipulations, and after an hour or so spent rummaging through a large carton of photographs of every possible style of house, from imitation medieval castles to run-down farm-houses, I settled on a roomy-looking former hunting-lodge covered with vines, and offering the possible shade of two beautiful mulberry trees, on either side of the friendly front lawn. I was attracted both by the house and the price, Fr. 4,000 per year, and the dealer was quite willing for me to take the photograph "to show to my husband," always a persuasive argument in France, no matter what is being negotiated.

◆ ◆ ◆

The house looked sufficiently isolated in the photograph for Gene to want to go see it, which we did, *en famille*. That is, Gene and I, with Betsy and her nurse, Armandine (the embittered divorced wife of a Dordogne druggist), and, just for the ride, Sherwood and Elizabeth Anderson who with their son John, were visiting in Paris.

There were no telephones in Colombey, except at the village doctor's, and I had written to the "best hotel," actually it was the only one, to reserve rooms for us, with special mention of the six-months' old baby. So, "Master, we were seven," when we boarded the train at the Gare de l'Est for Bar-sur-Aube, three hours from Paris, on a bright, cold winter morning, to see what awaited us.

To break the journey, Gene and the three Andersons decided to spend part of it in the dining-car. I stayed behind, having understood that the ex-*pharmacienne* was not a seasoned traveller, and might easily grow apprehensive if I too disappeared. She was in a talkative mood, and what more interesting topic could be found than our own travelling companions? "She looks very young, that lady (*cette dame*), to have a son as old as that young man." "Oh," I answered, "he is not her son; Mr. Anderson was married before." Then, idly enough I added, as an afterthought, "In fact, he was married twice before." Armandine's china-blue eyes narrowed suspiciously, and the red of her naturally florid cheeks deepened. "His wives?," she asked anxiously, "what did they die of?"

She had helped prepare drugs for the five thousand citizens of *Aire-sur-Adour.* She consequently knew all about arsenic and other such domestic poisons. "What did his wives die of?" she asked again. "Oh, I don't remember," I replied, "from just the ordinary natural causes, I suppose." But I don't believe that I succeeded in calming her fears. After all, she too, had followed the Landru case; she had no illusions: sometimes men did *awful* things! She remained deeply suspicious of Anderson. (I hope that she never heard about his two subsequent marriages, which made five.)

❖ ❖ ❖

The unheated hotel bedrooms were freezing cold, and we slipped quickly under the enormous red sateen feather-comfort (*couettes*), the trick being to keep it from slipping to the floor while you slept, when not so much as a cotton sheet would protect you from the icy blasts. Understandably, Betsy and Armandine had the privilege of the only heated room in the house, the bar-restaurant, and their beds were pulled close to the stove.

The next morning, having been served a copious *café-au-lait,* we left to visit *La Boiserie,* which we could see as we left the hotel, across a ravine of frozen gardens. The hotel-keeper, Monsieur Poulnot, who was custodian of the key, acted as guide.

After a short walk on a much-travelled dirt road lined with little individual peasant houses, we passed through an impressive gate between stone walls, that led down a gently sloping road to the former hunting-lodge (built *circa* 1850). On our left were tall old trees, underneath which was a veritable carpet, not of grass, but of closely-planted periwinkle that, later, was dotted with tiny flowers of a very special blue, half hidden under dark, shiny leaves. Shortly after we settled in the house, Gene discovered, deep under these leaves, a hare's nest with a mother and babies in it. Much to our sorrow, she soon became aware of our presence and left for a more secure shelter.

❖ ❖ ❖

The house stood in a clearing facing the village and, just as in the photograph, there were the two mulberry trees, stripped for winter, but giving promise of springs and summers to come. Behind the house was a wide open space of lawn with a few fruit trees, and up above, along the highroad wall, an avenue of lilac bushes. Close to the other end of the house, to break the wind from across a wide, sparsely populated valley, there was another cluster of tall old trees. The word Soupault used when he visited us was "austere." Perhaps. But it all looked very beautiful and desirable to us.

Architecturally, the house was a generous version of the "two pens and a passage" plan with, for good measure, a two-storey wing off the kitchen that eventually became, downstairs, a large pantry-storeroom and, upstairs, Gene's work-room, plus a small bed-room. The four large rooms, *i.e.,* the "pens," were spacious and light, and the main downstairs room had a vast open fireplace that separated the dining from the social end, where we put the grand piano. There were large windows at both ends of this room.

There was also an enormous attic that ran the whole length of the house, on the walls of which occupying troops, both French and American, had scrawled their messages: "Tomorrow *la perm* ("leave")!," or the names of girls and their attributes, what the young conscripts thought of certain officers. At least fifty recruits at a time could have been billeted in that attic.

The visit over, as we left the house, I noticed, in black stencilling on the stone wall over the door, the figure "4." M. Poulnot recalled that the American Army had numbered its houses. Where were Nos. 2 and 3? He didn't remember. After all, the war had ended nearly ten years earlier. Yes, the Marne river was not far distant. We did not insist.

Only later did we surmise that little M. Poulnot had probably been delegated to report what went on at *La Boisserie,* now that it was occupied by foreigners. He would turn up with no apparent motive; "Alors, Monsieur Jolas, ça va?" "Oui, oui, Monsieur Poulnot. Ça va. Sit down and let's have a drink." "Vous travaillez toujours, Monsieur Jolas?" "Oui, oui, toujours," Gene would answer jovially, and once this ritual accomplished, the old man had learned enough to make his report, transition was undoubtedly subversive but, in spite of our proximity to the Marne, I doubt if M. Poulnot's reports ever excited the suspicions of those who employed him.

❖ ❖ ❖

Already, on that first morning, we knew that we would come to live in this house, in spite of the fact that there was no electricity, no bathroom, a toilet that functioned with hand-carried water pitchers, and only one source of running water: in the kitchen. Although we were city-bred, these inconveniences seemed to us to be little more than just that, and undaunted, we signed a lease for three years, to start on April 15, 1927, with the hunter's daughter, Mme. Bombal, a charming, impoverished old lady.

❖ ❖ ❖

But I'm putting the cart before the horse, for there remained many loose ends to be gathered together in Paris before April 15th. These were, a): to find a Paris home for <u>transition</u> to which people could write and come, b): engage a second editorial assistant, c): engage a permanent assistant secretary to hold the fort in Paris.

The solution to problem *a* was an unusual one, but which proved to be both practical and satisfactory. The <u>transition</u> address: "40 rue Fabert, Paris VIIe," was the address of a small, family hotel in which I had once stayed. I had remained on friendly terms with the couple who owned it, as also with their daughter and her obliging young policeman husband.

The hotel faced the Place des Invalides—with a wide, unhampered view—and our fourth-floor "office," an erstwhile bedroom, of course, eventually became known to initiates from near and far. I recall that on the occasion of Marshal Foch's *funérailles nationales,* Joyce followed the long ceremony through a telescope, from the <u>transition</u> "office" window. He did not miss a trick, as readers of <u>Finnegans Wake</u> will have noticed.

Thanks to the proprietors, our voluminous post of "unsolicited manuscripts" was conscientiously handled and telephone messages noted. At times, too, the "cop" proved to be an extremely useful feature of this arrangement. After all, we were "foreigners," editing a magazine in a foreign language. What might we not be up to? He was always ready to vouch for us.

As for needs *b* and *c,* they too found satisfactory solutions: the very competent bilingual journalist, Robert Sage, also a "Chi-Trib" recruit, became a much appreciated editorial assistant, while his intelligent ex-wife, Maeve Sage, took over the Paris secretariat. The entire set-up was somewhat informal, but it satisfied our bicephalic requirements.

It was understood that Paul would come to occupy the single bed-room at "*La Boisserie,*" whenever close consultation became necessary. And the miracle was that he did come several times, and that we brought out twelve monthly issues during that first year, ten of which contained important fragments of Joyce's "Work in Progress." This represented no mean task, each installment involving as it did, for Gene, a personal visit, almost daily letters, several proofs, etc. For there were always changes to be made—usually additions, altered spellings, etc. But you couldn't lose patience with Joyce, even when on one occasion, the final O.K. of an entire issue had been given and binding had started. This time the addition was Joyce's reply—"The Mookes and the Gripes"—to an attack by Wyndham Lewis. We would not have wanted to miss that! Besides, Joyce was so courteous, so apologetic (however firm), that even the most adamant printers—usually autocrats themselves—acceded to his requests.

❖ ❖ ❖

As the first year drew to a close, Paul grew more evanescent, more difficult to pin down, his visits to Colombey more infrequent. Quite evidently too, he had other, very private fish to fry. So to our genuine regret, for he was both charming and competent, he faded out of transition's editorial picture. There were no hard feelings. Simply, one day we knew that he had bowed out. So we took his name off the mast-head and replaced him by Robert Sage.

That was in the Spring of 1928, No. 12 had appeared in March. On the title-page of No. 13, which came out that Summer, Paul was listed at the bottom of the page as "contributing editor," but I do not remember that he contributed regularly after No. 12. One result of his exit was the loosening of transition's ties to Gertrude Stein, contact with whom from the beginning, had been left to Paul, who was an admirer of hers and a frequent visitor to her house. In addition to her manuscripts for publication, Miss Stein was the source of some of the reproductions we published, notably, the Picasso cover for transition No. 13. All of these matters were handled through Paul, while, quite naturally, dealings with Joyce had fallen to Gene and me as had those with the Surrealists.

❖ ❖ ❖

After suspension in 1930 of the review's appearance when in 1932, Miss Stein heard of our plans to resume publication, she telephoned to ask us to publish her again, which we did, without enthusiasm.

Then, in 1934, her book Autobiography of Alice B. Toklas, was published in New York. In this book, written in her retarded-adolescent style, her countless mis-statements about practically everybody she had known in France, including Gene and me, in addition to her fatuous self-promotion, were so distasteful that I urged Gene immediately to reply to her mischievous misrepresentations with a refutation that would remain an essential document in all future discussions of this book as reliable history. The result was: "Testimony against Gertrude Stein," published as a 15 page supplement to transition No. 23 (1935), and containing the critical replies of: Georges Braque, Henri Matisse, André Salmon, Tristan

Tzara, and ourselves. Unfortunately, copies of this <u>Testimony</u> have all but disappeared from circulation. But it can, I believe, still be consulted here and there, and it should be consulted whenever Gertrude Stein's gratuitously inaccurate gossip is being cited.

I did not like Miss Stein, nor do I think that her talent was an important one; it was too artificial, too blatantly self-conscious and malicious for my taste. I shall, therefore, not return to the subject. My readers should know, however, the facts about her presence in Nazi France during the entire World War II. In 1946, in reply to my question: "How was it possible for Gertrude Stein, who was both American and Jewish, to live in comfortable, unmolested security during those five years, when Sylvia Beach, for instance, was arrested and spent six months in a detention camp merely because she was an American?" One of Stein's more naïf admirers answered: "She had very highly-placed protection."

Chapter VIII

As the months, then the seasons passed, each with its specific features more sharply experienced than in the city: in Winter, the wide expanses of snow, the leafless trees, the frozen ground; later, the barely perceptible, then sudden greening of the entire landscape; finally, the lush Summer and inevitable dying . . . All of these transformations contributed to an atmosphere of rhythmic peace that made Colombey each day more desirable to us both. Also, without realizing it, we had stumbled upon a forgotten pocket of what might be described, a bit hyperbolically perhaps, as latter-day "manorialism."

La Boisserie was the nearest thing to a "manor house" that had ever existed in this remote village, which actually, had only come into being because, some three centuries earlier, it had been the site of a relay-post, when stage-coach travel was extended to the Swiss and Rhenish borders. The village itself stood on a plateau, while down below, beside the main highway, vestiges of the XVIIth Century stables that had housed the replacement horses, could still be seen.

Colombey—had it ever really possessed two churches? Nobody seemed to know for sure. But it had no doubt supplied an answer to the less spiritual needs of those early travellers for refreshment and repose. (One also likes to picture the French *émigrés* resting here as they fled eastward on this same road in the late XVIIIth Century.)

By the first quarter of the XXth Century, which was when we arrived, *La Boisserie* too had probably often provided a welcome answer to the need of the handful of villagers on the plateau to possess a certain amount of "cash," in addition to the products of their gardens and farmyards. This need was our good fortune: for as a result, we never lacked for competent "help" to run our primitively equipped house.

I remember a little old woman, Marie, who proposed her daily services as the answer to one problem only: that every evening there should be light. She kept the oil lamps clean and filled, trimmed the wicks and polished the globes. She also monitored the candle-sticks, inserting fresh candles when necessary, and not forgetting to return them to the night-tables on which they belonged, with a supply of matches to hand. The electric switch was not missed, nor was the water spigot, for here, in spite of its single source, water always seemed to find its way into each waiting pitcher or bucket. The same was true of fire-wood for the various fire-places and stoves; we were never cold. A bit shamefacedly I confess that, thanks to these friendly, able people, who knew what to do better than I did, I have rarely lived more pleasantly, or more comfortably.

As I re-read these pages on *Colombey-les-Deux-Eglises*—to dignify it by its full name—I realize that, whereas I have set the stage, I have presented few of the actors who peopled it.

Our first visitor—who actually helped unload the piano!—was Monsieur le Curé, a kindly, tubby Christian whom we came to know and like well. I remember a conversation that he and I had during which I tried to inject a harmless American touch into this, to me, somewhat archaic, austere society. We were discussing the younger generation. They were not numerous, but having two of their pretty young girls in my employ—one to cook and the other to clean—I had become aware that their opportunities to meet their "boy friends" were limited to dark nights under the hedges.

Glowingly I described to our visitor the social life of the average young American (1920–1930): friendly meetings at one another's homes with, usually, dancing to "gramophone" records and followed, perhaps, by a glass of lemonade. Monsieur le Curé listened attentively, but he seemed disturbed.

"Oui, Madame," he said finally. "I feel sure that our young people would enjoy that. But . . . ," he hesitated, ". . . who would pay for the lemonade?" How stupid of me! I hadn't thought of that. So the Colombey youth continued to meet under the hedges, as good a way as any other, I suppose, to guarantee the regular succession of the generations.

❖ ❖ ❖

Then there was Thérèse, the gardener. Yes, she's a woman, people told me, but she works like a man and always does a man's work. This was quite evident, and we soon became accustomed to seeing this skirted—I should say many-skirted gardener (it was known to all that she always wore *all* her skirts *all* the time), whose manipulations with hoe and spade gave such excellent results.

Thérèse was the sixtyish daughter of a father who, when he died, had been Mayor of Colombey for fifty years. She lived quite alone, and opened her door to no one (a fact that was known for miles around). At the general store, she would wait until the last customer was served; "*Servez Madame,*" she would say, her covered basket with its newspaper-wrapped bottle to be filled, hidden under a waist-long rusty, black cape.

Our mutually satisfactory relationship continued uneventfully until one hot July day in 1928, when Marie reported excitedly, "Thérèse isn't coming, she's sick."

"Who is caring for her?," I asked. Thérèse had refused to open her door more than a narrow crack and the charitable Mme. Poulnot had thrown meat to her through the crack, was Marie's reply.

The French reaction to such news could be, "my blood *n'a fait qu'un tour,* or roughly, "rushed through my veins." My American blood, however, had begun to boil. "WHAT?" I shouted, and I started to give orders. "Get Emile and Henri (two occasional male workers). Tell them to bring the little folding bed with the mattress, pillows and clean linen to Therese's house. Bring several large pitchers, brooms, a shovel, towels, soap. I'll meet them there." They had never before seen me in the rôle of adjutant. But they did as I said.

Together, the two men succeeded in forcing the door wide open. Thérèse lay paralyzed in one corner on a pile of unidentifiable rags, papers, etc., directly on the floor. This, however, is a manner of speaking, because the "floor" had become a flea-ridden amalgam of earth and excrement, reinforced—the way one speaks of "reinforced concrete"—with the metal frames (the French say *carcasses*) of countless umbrellas!

The men worked quickly and well, a fire was built in the yard to heat water, the bed was set up nearby, women appeared who knew how to wash the sick. Soon Thérèse lay washed and clean on a clean bed in front of her house while a circle of gaping on-lookers grew larger and more incredulous. Old Marie, the lamp-cleaner, summed up the situation: "If you organized a procession to carry the statue of the Holy Virgin through the countryside nobody would come. But tell people Thérèse's door is open and they come from miles around!"

The same day, on a telephone call from the village Doctor, an ambulance from the Chaumont hospital, 25 kms., further east, came to fetch her. She died there six months later, without having come "home" again. The date was 1928, the place three hours' train-ride from Paris. Poor proud Thérèse! She was the Mayor's daughter, her bottle and her squalor were her own affair. I visited her at the hospital but I think that she did not understand why, or even know who I was.

❖ ❖ ❖

After the natives, the foreigners; those whom, as in my childhood prayers, I shall call my "friends and relations," and who made the journey to Colombey to see us.

They were not numerous, and only three out of my list of seventeen names are still alive today, in September, 1982. These are Kay Boyle, Moune Gilbert and Philippe Soupault. Long may they live! My affectionate thoughts many times recall the others. These were: Gene's mother and father, his sister Maria and her husband, Célestin Dillenschneider, Laurence Vail, Jacques Jolas, Martha and Whit Burnett, Bravig Imbs, Stuart Gilbert, Marie-Louise Soupault, Harry and Caresse Crosby. Joyce, who was an essentially urban man, did not come. He was, however, omnipresent.

Finally, my own mother, who was so delighted with the place that she offered to make us a present of it. But although tempted, Gene's time "on the land" was up, a decision that may have slightly altered the course of French history, since Charles de Gaulle and the Lorraine Cross would have found another resting place. It is interesting to speculate where.

We lived in Colombey for two and one-half hard-working, happy years, which were also, at times, ecstatic years, when the lilacs and the periwinkles were both in bloom and Jacques Jolas was flooding the house with Debussy, Scarlatti, or Beethoven.

We had left the too distant Mayenne printer for the "Etablissements André Brulliard," in nearby St. Dizier, which the purchase of a second-hand Ford car had made easily accessible. Having been the recipient at the age of 19 of a Model T. Ford sports-car, gift of my father, its uncomplicated driving reflexes were the only ones I possessed, and the intervening years had made me so unsure of my capacity to learn new ones that, quite simply, after we left Colombey, I never again drove a car. But during our stay there there was hardly a day when I didn't take the wheel for this or that urgent errand.

André Brulliard was a pleasant, very competent printer, as were his associates, and although he probably thought we were slightly mad—certainly that our contributor James Joyce was—he treated us with the indulgence of a father of high-spirited adolescents.

We finally succeeded in getting a telephone—quite a feat—and the possibility of direct contacts between Paris, St. Dizier and Colombey were an improvement that lightened considerably the burden of inter-secretarial correspondence. There was also Joyce, who was a great telephoner. He was glad to have us at the other end of the wire, a situation that opened up for him infinite possibilities: correcting, cutting, adding, revising—the entire gamut of his afterthoughts was frequently dictated by telephone.

During the summer of 1940, when refugees from eastern France were fleeing south by the hundreds, I was walking one day on a road near St. Gérand-le-Puy, in the Allier department, that ran between two fields where men were working.

Suddenly, I heard shouts of "Madame! Madame!" I looked in the direction of the caller: "Are you calling me?" I asked. Cupping his hands to make his voice carry, the man shouted: "Aren't you Madame Jolas?" "*Oui!,*" I shouted back, "Yes, I am Madame Jolas."

Delighted, he identified himself: "It was me who installed your telephone when you lived in Colombey-les-Deux-Eglises." Unfortunately, we were separated by planted fields so I could do little to thank him except to shout back, "Merci! Merci! Merci mille fois! . . . Et . . . bon courage!" Ships that pass in the night.

◆ ◆ ◆

But I see that I am about to close the Colombey chapter while there are still things to be told. For instance, my trip to America in the Spring of 1928 to show my nearly two-year-old Betsy to my family. They found her exotic (speaking no English) and lovely, which she was.

However, the other aim of my two-fold American mission: *i.e.,* to negotiate publication of a volume of translated surrealist texts from transition, with reproductions of the work of surrealist painters—Masson, Ernst, Tanguy, Chirico, Magritte *et al*—found no takers. Practically all of the publishers I consulted, and there were a good half-dozen, had the same objection: "These French movements come and go, and then they are forgotten. This one would not appear to be of any more importance than the others." I was no doubt a poor salesman, Gene would have done better. I returned to France and Colombey empty-handed.

Two or three years later, however, the break-through came, if I recall rightly, *via* interest shown by the New York Museum of Modern Art, which was as it should have been. And over half a century later, Surrealism, its tenets, its adepts, its creators and their creations, both literary and plastic, had replaced in the minds of many, the more conventional writers and artists of the same period many of whom, today, are all but forgotten. One explanation might be that a number of outstanding French poets, prose-writers and painters of the 1920–1950 epoch—here, however, it must be recalled that the great "triumvirate" of painters: Picasso, Matisse and Braque, remained aloof from surrealism, as did Nicolas de Stael—were exposed, however briefly, to the vivifying influence of surrealist "discipline" which, in turn, had been marked by Freudian thinking (cf. their insistence on the importance of the dream as a creative source, as well as their interest in the subconscious). Even more important was their re-discovery of German Romanticism. Gene did not hesitate to call the surrealists the "Romantics of the XXth Century."

I myself would venture to say that, except for the daring use of popular speech by the meteoric, unique Louis-Ferdinand Céline—(probably less original than was thought at the time, however, <u>Ulysses</u> having been available in French translation for some years)—<u>Surrealism</u> which, under André Breton's direction, opened up creative regions that had remained largely unexplored; and later, in 1950, Nathalie Sarraute's bold programme for a Nouveau Roman,[45] which she had already projected in her 1939 volume of sketches entitled <u>Tropisms</u>, have constituted the two important literary innovations that have emerged thus far during this century in French literature.

To conclude this brief and no doubt very partial account of the French literary scene, as I saw it, I have not been impressed by the attempts on the part of the better-known <u>Tel Quel</u> writers (post-1945), to impose criticism and analyses of the "writer writing" as forms of creative literature, however brilliant their style.

But there is another feature of the surrealist movement that I have found interesting, which is, that because of the increasingly important homosexual rôle in French intellectual life, the traditional man–woman relationship, that has always been such a constant in French literature, seemed at one moment to have been relegated to a past epoch. <u>Surrealism</u> reinstated the love of men for women —if only for "*la femme enfant,*" and I recall that one of its more famous manifestos: "Hands off Love," (<u>transition</u> No. 6, September, 1927), was written in support of Charles Chaplin, who at that time, was the victim of attacks by rampant U.S. puritanism. As is well known, Chaplin later married 17 year-old Oona O'Neill, and "they lived happy ever after," blessed with a numerous progeny. André Breton was married three times. And when, after his death in 1966, his biographer, Marguerite Bonnet, "defended" her Doctor's thesis on his first twenty years, before a Sorbonne jury, not only his widow, but both his former wives were present.

After this lengthy and, I fear, barely legitimate digression, during which I have remained suspended between New York and Paris, I must nevertheless return briefly to Colombey before leaving it for good. The birth there of my second daughter, Marie Christine (Tina), remains to be told. The date was an ideal June 10, 1929, and lest I forget, never was the month of June more deserving of its reputation: "month of roses," than was that June of 1929. Everywhere one looked, on every wall, in each garden, there were roses and more roses to welcome my baby.

Plans had been made for her (or him) to arrive, as Betsy had, in Paris, where she (or he) would be ushered into the world by the same tall ex-Polish Norman,

---

45. With the support of Alain Robbe-Grillet, Michel Butor, Claude Simon and Robert Pinget.

Dr. Powilowicz. That was in the morning, by telephone from *La Boisserie*. We would take a late afternoon train for Paris. But as we all know, man can do no more than "propose," whereas God, nature and unborn babies are the ones who eventually "dispose." This time all three had decided differently.

The day passed quietly, devoted for the most part to planning my absence. An hour before train time Gene and I kissed Betsy good-bye and headed for Bar-sur-Aube in the Ford. We picked up the freshly laundered baby-clothes on our way.

But soon I began to recognize certain unmistakable symptoms that were becoming increasingly insistent. Perhaps, before undertaking the three-hour train trip, I would do well to consult a local doctor. He was categorical: "You can't possibly go to Paris." He telephoned my Paris doctor, (to whom he added the arcane mention: "five francs") and engaged a room at the local hospital. In less than an hour, I was comfortably settled in a pleasant room with, in a crib beside me, a newly-arrived daughter born, like the French philosopher, Gaston Bachelard, in Bar-sur-Aube.

Actually, I was fortunate, for the Bar-sur-Aube hospital had no obstetrical facilities, and they had kindly accepted me in their recently opened surgical wing. A feature of this hospital was that it also housed a "hospice," in this case, a home for indigent old men.

The days passed happily. Gene's daily visits were particularly appreciated by the inmates of the *hospice,* who soon understood that there was a chain-smoker who dropped countless cigarette butts from the open window of an upstairs room. The news also spread quickly through the nursing force (some fifty nuns) that an American lady had given birth there and that, too, constituted a minor "event." I was numerously visited, questioned—from Kentucky? Where is that? etc. Why had I come to France? A singer! Ah . . . sing something for us. And I have a memory of being propped up on several pillows while I sang the "Jewel song" from <u>Faust</u>—neither more nor less—to an audience composed of the Mother Superior and a bevy of nuns gathered on either side of my bed.

But after all, I was American. Sing something American. So I obliged with <u>Old Kentucky Home</u>, <u>Swanee River</u>, etc. They understood not a word, of course, but they did seem, nevertheless to recognize the difference between Marguerite's mirrored triumph as imagined by Goethe and Gounod, and the anonymous "ladies," urged to "weep no more" by the more modest American composer, Stephen Collins Foster.

◆ ◆ ◆

"Lying-in," at that time, being an affair of two to three weeks, I had ample time to get to know the little nun who was assigned to me. She had been to Paris and remembered the Place de la Concorde. How beautiful it was! Once we spoke of her vows: chastity, poverty, obedience. Which one, I asked indiscreetly, was the hardest to observe? I have often thought of her reply. "These three are not difficult," she said. "The hardest thing in our lives is "*le support mutuel*" (mutual forbearance).

She gave a recent example of this problem: each time she had tarried in my room to chat after supper, the next morning, at breakfast, a sister nun never failed to inquire obliquely after my health. Had she really been obliged to stay that late? was what had been implied.

Fortunately, the handsome, authoritative Mother Superior was well able to control both the open and the hidden tensions by which her flock of fifty could have been perturbed and their professional competence marred. This was my first glimpse into the inner functioning of a small, tightly held, all-female community, a situation that I often recalled some years later, when I myself became head of a small private school, a position that involved peace-keeping among pupils, parents and personnel. "Mutual forbearance"—how essential, and yet how difficult to achieve!

On our return to Colombey, there was a proper baptism in the village church, which was accompanied by such arduous ringing of bells that for months, and for miles around, wherever I went, I was congratulated, sometimes by total strangers, on the widely heard celebration of my baby's introduction to Christian ritual: "*Ah! c'est vous la maman!* How the bells rang!" I did not tell them, that Gene had so generously greased the palm of the already happy bell-ringer that he seemed to feel duty-bound to furnish a double ration of joyful sound.

But neither holy baptism nor jubilation altered the fact that the object of this celebration, Tina, was destined to become a hard-to-raise baby, for a reason which, today, would be recognized as legitimate: she had an organic intolerance for milk, an idiosyncrasy the very existence of which had not yet been generally recognized by French pediatricians. In fact, the latter were themselves, still a rare species at that time, when medical supervision of a baby's first year was generally entrusted to the obstetrician. Mine had but one suggestion to make in reply to my anxious accounts of this poor baby's rejection of both breast and bottle: "Madame," he would say kindly, "you must insist." This I did. But it was borne in on me each day more clearly that this was not the calm, easy child that Betsy had been.

◆ ◆ ◆

The summer passed uneventfully and we were facing another winter. Gene was becoming restless and anxious. The new baby was delicate, he himself was obliged to go more frequently to Paris. We would do best to leave Colombey. For where?

Not *in* Paris. But not far from Paris, either. I began to study the "for-rent" ads. My eye lighted upon a suitable house and small garden, within our price range, in Enghien, twelve minutes from the Paris Gare du Nord. And by Autumn's end, we had left Colombey for the rather stuffy little race-course town. We did not return to Colombey until some five or six years later, when a nostalgic impulse moved Gene to show the children where we had lived.

Monsieur Poulnot greeted us like old friends. Yes, the house was still unoccupied but it had only recently been sold. To whom? To "some colonel or other,"[46] was his laconic reply, as a home for his ailing daughter. For Gene and me all kinds of happy memories were revived by that visit. I doubt if the little girls retained any other than that of a gay family outing.

◆ ◆ ◆

A quarter-century later the address: Colombey-les-Deux-Eglises, Haute Marne, was to become famous as the home of General Charles de Gaulle, who spent his years of retirement and died there (1970), in the house we—and transition— had occupied for nearly three years.

Journalists, recognizing a syllable they knew in the name *La Boisserie,* explained blithely to their readers, that the place had once been a brewery, although there is no water within miles! Actually, I was told by the proprietor that the name derived quite simply from *Bois,* woodland, there being many wooded areas nearby where such big game as wild boar and even deer may be found. After all, the house was built as a "hunting-lodge." The "Bois de la lune," which stretches between *La Boisserie* and the well-known Clairvaux prison, was also often referred to in connection with occasional escaped convicts, those desperate quarry for hunters of even bigger game.

◆ ◆ ◆

After the General moved in, a three-storey tower in which were housed his administrative services, was added to the west wall. The village became the mecca for many prominent political figures seeking authoritative wisdom; the need for reinforced security measures eventually transformed the gentle old place into a miniature police-state. I doubt if for many years, a mother hare again hid her babies under the periwinkles.

The General is buried beside his daughter, in the village churchyard, and an immense Lorraine cross dominates the surrounding countryside. After Verdun,

---

46. Little did I dream then that ten years later, this obscure Colonel would have become the revered leader in a cause—to free France from Nazism—that would enlist my own ardent political activism.

Colombey has become another goal of patriotic pilgrimage for those Frenchmen who want to honour this lonely giant, who said "no" to Nazism, when so many of his compatriots said "yes."

And, more modestly, I like to think that, scattered throughout the English-speaking world, there are others for whom Colombey was also once the home and work-shop of transition.

Journal Draft about the Events of 1932 and l'Ecole Bilingue
(December 8, 1982)

The two years [1930–32] we spent in the Rue de Sévigné were a time of lights and shadows. Tina continued to be a delicate child, with a tendency to what was startlingly diagnosed, at the time, as bronchial pneumonia, and, much later, more accurately, as asthma. At those moments, Joyce's anxiety was closely tuned to our own, and I have not forgotten his constant solicitude. He knew, as few do, the real meaning of what, in German, is called *mitleid,* suffering with, and when his own time for intense suffering came, it was essential for him that his friends should share his pain.

Those were the years when Lucia's condition could no longer be explained as simply erratic; specialists consulted were becoming more explicit; Joyce rejected their diagnoses impatiently, and was soon making his own, for which he recommended improbable cures: her artistic talents should be given greater recognition, she should visit Ireland, where she would be among his own people, etc. etc. Some of them were tried, but in vain.

Dear Joyce! He also resolutely rejected the diagnosis: "schizophrenia" which, at that time, was of uncertain origin and treatment, although it was the conclusion of most of the specialists consulted both in France and in Switzerland. Nora was more fatalistic; early on, she did not foresee a cure. That was in 1932. I am writing this, a few days after Lucia's death, at the age of 75, on Dec. 12, 1982.

◆ ◆ ◆

The next move—to Neuilly, a suburb just West of Paris—was not due this time to Gene's desire for change. Betsy had reached school-age, what solution would we choose? I was already viscerally opposed to the rigours and unrelieved seriousness—no singing or dancing, no handwork or dramatics—nothing but lessons and more lessons, that were said to characterize French schools of that time, even in the smaller classes. We wanted School to be a happy time. After all, hadn't we, in our Declaration of Independence, been told that each citizen had an "inalienable right" to the "pursuit of happiness"? Betsy should not be deprived of this right.

Then one day, quite by chance, I ran into an American friend, Fanny Ventadour, who had children about the age of mine. She told me of the blissful days that her children were spending in a "play-school," in Neuilly, that had been organized by [Mrs. Haynes,] the wife of an American business-man stationed in Paris. This energetic and intensely American mother had imported a trained American teacher, rented an old-fashioned two-story house with a large garden and engaged two Russians: a man of all work and a cook, a jovial variously gifted grandmother, who had escaped by her wits from revolutionary disruption in order to give her very young orphaned granddaughter a more stable future. Finally, my energetic compatriot had engaged a perfectly bilingual teacher: Mrs. Hermine Priestman. She was the daughter of Auguste Bréal, granddaughter of Michel Bréal (who first used the term "la linguistique"). Her husband, the father of her four children, who were aged if I remember rightly 7, 6, 4, and 3,—was of British stock. All four children were already naturally bilingual, a fact that, with my two, constituted a good base from which to start our experiment of bilingual teaching. Although [I] first called the school *L'Ecole bilingue de Neuilly,* [it] soon became known in Paris "Nouvelle Education" circles as *L'Ecole Bilingue,* a title that was since the war has been adopted by a different group and, I believe, has filled a need felt by many Paris parents, conscious of the advantage of possessing not only a second language, but as in the case of 20th century English, a universal language.

In spite of the long subway ride from our Rue de Sévigné to Neuilly—12 stations plus a 20 minute walk—we decided to accept the challenge of a situation that, although far from perfect, would keep Betsy the American citizen we had wanted her to be when we very early registered her at the U.S. Embassy in Paris.

In the beginning, in 1932, the school seemed larger than necessary. But it grew. We shall pass rapidly through the ensuing years. In October 1935, we rented a more spacious building, at no. 60 of the Rue Borghèse, on the same street where we already were, with a tennis court, a large garden, and sunny classrooms. From the little Ecole Nouvelle de Neuilly, we became the Ecole Bilingue, officially a French school, a dependency of the Academy of Paris. All our personnel spoke English fluently, but the courses were given in French, and all the teachers were French except myself, and I didn't teach.

A second building was added in October 1938, still on the Rue Borghèse. By June, 1939, we had 145 students of different nationalities: French, English,

American, German, Russian, Spanish, etc. An atmosphere of gaiety and youth prevailed. I began thinking about adding still another building: As a woman of action I organized myself as usual. On the 10th of August, I left for Savoy for a few weeks of vacation with my family, confident in the future.

And yet I was less confident than I seemed. The human spirit is a funny thing. And beside my attitude of wishful thinking, quite a few thoughts were taking a different direction—evacuation in case of a declaration of war. Subsequent to several conversations with a student's mother, who had suggested to me her own property in the center of France as a place to fall back on—I had in fact communicated the address to all the students' families and to the school personnel. But I didn't believe in or want the war. Why think about death when life is calling in such an insistent fashion?

September 1939. We had just taken the little train to go up to St. Gervais, in the Savoy. My husband was sitting by my side, very solemn. Our two little girls and a little friend were gaily chattering, unconscious, happy in this lovely day. "The white papers (the mobilisation sheets) are posted," my husband whispered to me: "It's war." "Is it inevitable?" I asked. "But of course, now it can't end any other way." Up there, just at the foot of the Mont Blanc glacier, the world in such commotion seemed so small, so silly, that I couldn't remember these things. The three children were weaving flower wreaths while my husband and myself were listening hour after hour to the radio of the inn. No hope! Even the gaiety of the children seemed already to belong to a finished world that we'd never be seeing again. Coming back in the evening, in the little train, a young couple was exchanging amorous glances, sadly, with a disheartened air that will always remain in front of my eyes like the symbol of so many young loves, young hopes all over Europe, who, during these tragic days of August 1939 saw their happiness fleeing, probably for long years to come.

Two days later all the hotels of St. Gervais were empty, the streets unlit. The reign of darkness, not to say of obscurantism had begun in Europe.

I shall simply sketch out briefly the life of the Bilingual School as it was evacuated to Bourbonnais, 18 kilometers from Vichy, in what was to be, after the invasion, unoccupied territory. It became a completely different school from that of Neuilly—a boarding school instead of a day school, and 45 students instead of 145—almost all the Americans and British had left the country at the outbreak of war—and a staff of 7 instead of 22. But there were major compensations: life in the country perfectly suited all our students, and for myself I consider that experience as a rich addition to what I had already learned concerning education.

During those autumn months, and still during the summer harvest, the children helped the peasants in their farm work—each class kept up a garden. They watched with bated breath as the woodcutters cut down an enormous oak, never had the natural history classes been so lively, and I understood, we all understand, that here the child is in his element, feeling truly at home.

As months passed—these months of war with no war—we almost had an illusion of happiness. But in the depths of each grownup heart the idea of the menace hanging over us lingered, except that the idea of defeat was not yet born. With the 10th of May the menace arrived, and scarcely a month after came defeat, this defeat which had seemed impossible to all of us.

One evening, in their bathrobes around the radio, our pupils listened to the venerable soldier, the one who could have been their great grandfather say: "Frenchmen: we have lost the battle. A large part of our territory will be occupied; our prisoners will remain prisoners until the end of the war with England. We have wanted an easy life, now we have suffering. Let us go to work, let us build a new France on the foundation of its ancient virtues. France cannot die."

Silently the pupils left the room to go to bed. The next day, and how many times after, you could see them discussing the future of their dear country, in little groups. Sometimes they didn't speak of it, and I am certain that the blade had entered their hearts, and that these children, during these tragic moments they lived, were dedicating themselves never to rest, until France would be born again, lovelier than ever.

Then our students left little by little during the summer months. Little by little the anguished families were able to come to us—most of the time on bicycle —and before my departure from Vichy, on August 28, 1940, the last pupil was with his family, the last textbooks were put up in an attic, waiting until the school could open once more. With a heavy heart and almost without any hope at all I said farewell—not even *au revoir*—to a work that since 1932 had passionately interested me, permitting me an intimate knowledge of nearly a thousand children.

The Revolution of the Word Proclamation, 1929

PROCLAMATION

TIRED OF THE SPECTACLE OF SHORT STORIES, NOVELS, POEMS AND PLAYS STILL UNDER THE HEGEMONY OF THE BANAL WORD, MONOTONOUS SYNTAX, STATIC PSYCHOLOGY, DESCRIPTIVE NATURALISM, AND DESIROUS OF CHRYSTALLIZING A VIEWPOINT . . .

WE HEREBY DECLARE THAT:

1. THE REVOLUTION IN THE ENGLISH LANGUAGE IS AN AC-COMPLISHED FACT.

2. THE IMAGINATION IN SEARCH OF A FABULOUS WORLD IS AUTONOMOUS AND UNCONFINED.

> *(Prudence is a rich, ugly old maid courted by Incapacity* . . . Blake)

3. PURE POETRY IS A LYRICAL ABSOLUTE THAT SEEKS AN A PRIORI REALITY WITHIN OURSELVES ALONE.

> *(Bring out number, weight and measure in a year of dearth* . . . Blake)

4. NARRATIVE IS NOT MERE ANECDOTE, BUT THE PROJEC-TION OF A METAMORPHOSIS OF REALITY.

> *(Enough! Or Too Much!* . . . Blake)

5. THE EXPRESSION OF THESE CONCEPTS CAN BE ACHIEVED ONLY THROUGH THE RHYTHMIC "HALLUCINATION OF THE WORD." (Rimbaud).

6. THE LITERARY CREATOR HAS THE RIGHT TO DISINTE-GRATE THE PRIMAL MATTER OF WORDS IMPOSED ON HIM BY TEXT-BOOKS AND DICTIONARIES.

> *(The road of excess leads to the palace of Wisdom* . . . Blake)

7. HE HAS THE RIGHT TO USE WORDS OF HIS OWN FASHION-ING AND TO DISREGARD EXISTING GRAMMATICAL AND SYN-TACTICAL LAWS.

> *(The tigers of wrath are wiser than the horses of instruction* . . . Blake)

8. THE "LITANY OF WORDS" IS ADMITTED AS AN INDEPEN-DENT UNIT.

9. WE ARE NOT CONCERNED WITH THE PROPAGATION OF SOCIOLOGICAL IDEAS, EXCEPT TO EMANCIPATE THE CREATIVE ELEMENTS FROM THE PRESENT IDEOLOGY.

10. TIME IS A TYRANNY TO BE ABOLISHED.

11. THE WRITER EXPRESSES. HE DOES NOT COMMUNICATE

12. THE PLAIN READER BE DAMNED.

(Damn braces! Bless relaxes! . . . Blake)

—*Signed*: KAY BOYLE, WHIT BURNETT, HART CRANE, CARESSE CROSBY, HARRY CROSBY, MARTHA FOLEY, STUART GILBERT, A. L. GILLESPIE, LEIGH HOFFMAN, EUGENE JOLAS, ELLIOT PAUL, DOUGLAS RIGBY, THEO RUTRA, ROBERT SAGE, HAROLD J. SALEM-SON, LAURENCE VAIL.

"The Revolution of the Word Proclamation" as it appeared in *transition* 16/17, 1929.

War Diary, 1940
(excerpts)

Tuesday, June 25, 1940
Unforgettable week of anguish, fear, humiliation, relief, calm—the calm of complete resignation in a state that could not more nearly resemble death and not be death.

[Looking back] *Sunday 16th*
Paris fell on Friday.

Joyces came in the morning, their hotel being requisitioned in Vichy ... My own fatigue after a night passed at the St.-Germain Station, trying to help the countless, miserable refugees. The spoiled American woman weeping on the quai because she had been asked to leave her hotel in Vichy. Her pile of hatboxes. Her fear she might not reach Bergerac in time to find her daughter. How I scolded her! The countless frightened Jews. The little sales-girl with her mother and beautiful baby ("she's been coddled all her life.") The exhausted people sleeping in tiers in the military dormitory. My crippled old woman from Dijon who, at the first bombardment, had fled, didn't know where she was headed for. The two young women with babies, large bundles, two grandmothers, one who fell unconscious on the floor of the train, on her knees, as we hurriedly lifted her in. The charming, high-bred, Dominican nuns and the courtesy that everyone accorded them. The trainloads of cannon and other materials, soldiers sleeping on them. Cattle cars with soldiers and civils together. One car of young soldiers playing a harmonica; chalked on the car "Les privés d'amour." The courtesy of the railway employees, the people sleeping in piles on the floor of the platforms. A terrible, distressing spectacle. A people en exode, la grande peur.

Monday June 17th Classes as usual.
In the night the Reynaud government had fallen. . . . Pétain had taken it over. 2 am the voices in the courtyard. 5 am. French officers asking for *essence.* Claude, the gardener, received them. *"Je ne pouvais pourtant pas leur pisser de l'essence dans leurs réservoirs."* ("After all, I couldn't piss gas into their tanks.")

The Germans are in the Yonne, the Germans are at Nevers, the Germans are in Moulins. Where were they now? Would they come here? If they did what would we do? Will they carry off the big boys? They say that's what they have done everywhere. What of the men? Had anybody a bicycle? Groups were forming in all the villages. Where would they go? Nobody knew. Away, out of reach of the invader. The cars poured by, all going South. Mattresses attached to the roofs—household effects, children frightened, exhausted people. Paris autobuses, Auteuil, Passy, etc.

German soldiers in the square, in the shops, in the cafés, everywhere. They quickly bought up all the things no longer to be found in Germany—a little jeweler's shop emptied of everything, paid for in paper marks—yards of woolen material to be sent back to their families etc.etc. The attitude of the population of St. Gérand was not always perfect. Children on the square played with the soldiers, a young woman said all she wanted was that her husband should return, she didn't care if she became *boche*. There was much admiration of the uniforms and their orderly way of doing things, etc. etc. At one café a young woman lifted her champagne glass to theirs. Nervousness, relief that they were not before brutes who pillaged, burnt, etc. (as they had feared to be). It is difficult to explain this reaction. The older generation on the other hand understood the tragedy of the moment and remained in quiet dignity *chez eux*.

The days passed, heavy, nameless. Time hung like the albatross about our necks. 8:30, 11:30, 12:30, 1:30, 4:30, 6:30, 7:00, 9:30, 10:30, 11:30. We missed none of the French government radio broadcasts. "*Aux Armes Citoyens! Ici le Poste National de l'Etat Français. Prière d'écouter l'émission du Radio Journal de France.*" That was around June 12th. What could Roosevelt answer? On the roads old peasants met me: "Madame, we count on your president. Oh, Madame, don't you think he can help us?" My heart sank at all this naiveté, beginning with that of Reynaud. He knew then that it was a matter of hours for France, of weeks, perhaps months for the United States. What a fruitless dramatic gesture.

Then had come the fatal night of June 14th. Paris had fallen that day. "M. Paul Reynaud vous parle." Reynaud's voice came, heavily dramatic, through the air. Almost too much so, I felt. There seemed a lack of simplicity, a lack of the extraordinary dignity that we heard in Pétain's voice later on.

"Against a great superior number in persons and weapons, our valiant army . . . We are going to suffer. Let us be brothers. Losing this battle. . . . France will rise again."

I remained alone with Marthe, the old French aristocrat, as much a part of the soil as the very root of the grape. "Where are the English? Where are they?" I suddenly felt very much of an outsider, guilty of something that had been left undone. Her only son in the turmoil, everything else lost. I sought some word of comfort.

We shall surely come, Marthe. England will keep on fighting, we will send material as fast as possible, in fact we've already sent lots of aeroplanes, etc. and then France will be restored. Surely it will be like that, I said. It can't be otherwise. But you must understand what my country is, you must understand how slowly we move; how undermined we have been by German propaganda.

But my words brought no comfort. On the contrary. "The United States will help England! And France, they have let her roll over and die, like a dog." Thanks to her deep faith, this mood of revolt did not last. But I saw through her the consternation and despair of the real France before a disaster such as, since Jeanne d'Arc, the country had never known.

Pétain, the venerable old man, came before the microphone: "Frenchmen!" how different from the cello voice of M. Reynaud. "We have lost; a large part of our country will be occupied until the war with England is over, nearly ten million of our people are refugees in conditions of intense distress. I hate lies. You have already heard too many. Our life will be hard. We have preferred pleasure to work and we are now before suffering. Your government will move to a point in central France from which it will do all in its power to alleviate the sufferings, to reorganize the lives of our citizens. France cannot die!"

The Marseillaise! Everyone stands. All gravely silent, some weeping quietly. The children went to bed. The adults lingered a bit for a few hushed comments, then followed them. For the fatigue of those overcharged days had been terrible. And that day, Wednesday, had been declared a day of mourning in all France.

Aside from the heart-rending spectacle of the civil refugees, that of the military refugees is, if anything, even more heart-rending. Hundreds of young men on bicycles, their poor things tied up in a blanket, dressed in whatever civil attire they might find, wearily, disgruntledly, often, trying to elude the German authorities, trying to return to their families. The defeat had made them sore and many tell the tale of officers who "turned tail," who left them to shift for themselves. The impression may be wrong, doubtless it is, for the French officer is neither a coward nor a cad, but there is no doubt but that the German pressure on land and overhead was so terrifying that it was impossible for any large group of men and material to stay together. The result was a veritable confusion such as has not been witnessed since Waterloo.

At school the 20 odd children who are left are working, under guidance, of course, on a natural history museum of the region. They are keen about it and already have a collection of woods, butterflies, tadpoles, etc., that is very imposing. We are having classes in the morning as nobody knows what to do while waiting for the possibilities of dispersion, and in the afternoon the children have time to work on the museum, sports, etc.

The weather is mild and sunny, the flowers are all in bloom and one is sometimes tempted to forget, under the spell of the great trees, that this is a defeated, unhappy land faced with hunger and misery. For hunger is the part of thousands here today. There is a shortage of all good supplies and it is hard to see just how the problem will be solved. We go from farm to farm for butter, potatoes, etc. and are lucky to find anything, particularly potatoes, which are a great rarity. As for coal there is none and I wonder how long I can find food and cook it for my 50 people. Perhaps the fact that the government has come to Vichy will facilitate this. On the other hand the contrary effect is also possible. Fortunately I had good stocks of dry groceries and one garden is beginning to yield. Meat is scarce, however and there are no fruits to be had. We killed a pig last week and put it in the *saloir*. The *boudin* and *filets* were a treat.

Another sad tale. Hitler will free all Alsatian and Lorraine prisoners. Why? To go where? To do what?

Sometimes I feel oppressed by the politically conscious feature of man's intelligence. *Boche* or not, is not the earth the same as it was under countless other regimes? The trees, the sky itself? Could not these things suffice? I know of course that they could not, that even these supposedly immutable parts of a country can be poisoned by the political atmosphere that obtains there. But one is tempted when this itching becomes intolerable to see a real identity with nature, to lose one's self in her universal kindliness.

Today will be a momentous day in French history. The French parliament—18 kilometers away—voted its own dissolution and practically put the entire life of the county in the hands of Maréchal Pétain—aged 81!—who, with Laval as Président du Conseil will govern on dictatorial lines. This is surely a transition government, for Pétain's age makes anything else impossible.

Oh what a moral lesson it has all been! Defend, defend aggressively all that we love and value! How little I understood these things before.

Letter to Her Friends in France, April 28, 1941

(excerpts)

I have made copies of these pages for all my friends in France. I'd be hard put to it to explain to you the terrible exhaustion I have felt at writing letters since I've arrived here. It's a form of fatigue and interior distress that I already knew, and somewhat the result of a great physical and moral effort, which has lasted a long time.

I should add that much of my time this year has been devoted to my friends the Joyces, for whom I have been trying to do something here since October. The death of James Joyce himself deprives us of a very rare and irreplaceable friend, and adds a great deal to the sorrows brought about by events. The world of letters laments his absence everywhere, in friendly and enemy countries: but that's a meager consolation for those who loved him so much!

Let me recount our odyssey:

After a wait in Cerbère that was never sufficiently explained, we missed our ship two weeks in a row, so that we got to New York only on the 28 of September: two days at a hotel, some days in the countryside with friends, then a return to New York, again at the hotel; the children will enter the Lycée right away and I began to look for a furnished apartment in the neighborhood. Alas, they are all too expensive, and so I started looking around for an unfurnished one. After ten days, we found 5 rooms, relatively calm, a bit of sun in the morning, on the ninth floor about fifteen minutes by foot from the school. . . .

Scarcely had we unpacked when people started asking me for translations of French lectures. I've translated more than a hundred and fifty literary pages; I had to help my husband with other translations, and since I've been here, I've given four lectures on your country: two in my birthplace, one in New York, before 150 former students of my school and one before six hundred students in the State of Iowa. You can be sure that I've done what I possibly could so that people will understand and love France in this moment of terrible trial. The misunderstanding of events had been rather great; it still is, but the affection that every American feels for France hasn't been harmed—that's the main thing.

The greatest problem for me has been that of the children's adapting to their new life. Betsy has shown herself full of scholarly zeal and very anxious to do well everything demanded of her. She's working seriously at her piano, and her music teacher is very satisfied with her progress. But her heart has remained in France. She is rather somber, closed in upon herself. Tina reacts otherwise, sleeping badly, working badly, becoming bossy, angry, even insolent and at the same time rather negative, avoiding any effort. Now things are better.

After Tina, Claude, little Claude Duthuit [Matisse's grandson], who has been part of our family this year. He's a charming and affectionate child, who has adjusted—or seems to have—to his new life. For alas, he is very distracted, often makes trouble in class, and his relationship with the *lycée* has not been very satisfactory. As with the two others, the three or four first months were the hardest.

The material problem is weighing on us, as odd as that may seem. The trip was costly, life is very expensive here, and we are no doubt on the threshold of a rather great economic crisis. On the psychological side, I see that in those who are no longer young there is a great confusion, resulting from such an uprooting, originating in such grave events that can paralyze you; I feel it myself, even as an American returning to my own country where I still have relationships, and, Dieu merci! some modest resources. So I have the greatest sympathy for the real refugees, who without knowing our language and without any money, come here all the same in the hope of a better future; may their hopes be realized!

Here in New York and also in Canada, there are now some French publishing houses and we've been able to read some very good books. But the penury of French books in the *lycée* for example, means that they have to mimeograph the textbooks.

The telephone never stops ringing, and the days fly by. Someone needs shoes; have you counted the linen? The butcher's check, the translation I promised, the proofs of this article, the meetings of the "Joyce Memorial Fund Committee" whose chairman I am; the door—my nephew, my brother, a sister, a friend, and yourself? What do you look like, with your shoelaces all used up, your hair in strings, your old dress?

The days go by, and as for me, never does the thought of France and the French, especially of all of you whom I love so, ever leave us. You are collectively the constant preoccupation of millions of people here.

I firmly believe in a better day to come, and that we will see each other again in very different conditions from those I left. Let's keep this faith.

Radio Address, May 3, 1941

Text of a radio address delivered by Mrs. Eugene Jolas
Station WCNH (Brooklyn) May 3, 1941
under the auspices of

THE FIGHT FOR FREEDOM COMMITTEE

The microphone is such an anonymous form of communication that, before I attack my subject this evening, I am going to take a few moments to tell you something of my own background; in other words, justify to you my right to appear before this microphone on behalf of the "Fight for Freedom Committee."

I am an American citizen, born in this country. On both my Father's and my Mother's side, the date of 1750 found my ancestors already settled in Virginia. I do not speak to you, therefore, either as a European or even as a recent European, but simply as an American who has lived for many years in Europe. Curiously enough, too, I am the first of my line after nearly two hundred years on this continent, to have felt at home on the European continent.

In 1913 I went to Berlin as a student of singing and I spent nearly a year in the German capital. At the end of the first World War, which interrupted my studies in Germany, I returned to Europe, this time to Paris, and again as a student of singing. I lived 21 years in France, that is to say, from 1919 to 1940. During those years, I married an American citizen of more recent European ancestry than my own—his parents were from Lorraine and the Rhineland—and my children were born in France.

As they grew to school age I founded a franco-american school in Paris, called the Bilingual School, which was a flourishing organisation until war came. In September 1939, after the declaration of war, being fearful of a possible bombing of Paris, I moved my school to a country district in the center of France, not far from the sleepy watering-place that has since become a symbol for all that is tragic and equivocal in our time, Vichy. In that lovely rolling country, flanked by the Bourbonnais hills and traced with graceful little rivers where, according to the regional guide-books, "no enemy foot had ever trod," I was to witness an event which, despite all that had gone before in other parts of Europe, I would have called entirely fantastic a month earlier.

It was here that the invasion of France, in June 1940, found me, it was here, too, that I passed the rest of that fateful summer, for I did not return to this country until late September. And so I speak to you to-night as an American whose experiences have included a re-discovery of the civilisation to which our own civilisation owes so much, and who, having witnessed Europe's terrible fate at the hands of a ruthless barbarian horde am fearful for our own beloved America. For unlike Colonel Lindbergh, who finds no other persons responsible for the present situation in Europe than a group in each country he calls "interventionists," I accuse the Nazi Führer, the Nazi party and, behind them, every German in Germany and throughout the world who has taken part in and condoned this series of crimes that has brought misery and distress to millions. In France and England, yes, there were, if you want, "interventionists," that is to say, people who felt that having given their word to Poland, they must intervene. But I defy Colonel Lindbergh, or Hitler himself, to name any persons who might have been called "interventionists" in Austria, Czecho-Slovakia, Denmark, Norway, Holland, Belgium and Luxembourg. No, a thousand times no, these countries were *violated,* as any one of the hundreds of their citizens who are in this country can assure you.

The number of Americans who witnessed the fall of France must be around 4000, and it is interesting to note that nearly all of us, beginning with his Excellency Ambassador Bullitt, are trying, each in his way, to bring to our own compatriots the same message: America, awake! This is not England's war alone. It is the war of every man and woman to whom a free life is essential. As a noted French writer has expressed it: this is a war between slave-owners and abolitionists.

In the winter of 1939, I listened one day to Premier Daladier speaking by radio to the French people. "Fellow countrymen," he said, "let us not forget that however unlike other wars this one may appear to be, we are, as before, defending the soil of France." My own thought, on hearing this was: "Of course he does well to tell them this but, obviously, this time it is not true." For I also listened to the German radio each evening and I heard the countless reassurances addressed to France from across the Rhine—in the purest French, alas—as to Germany's real attitude towards the French people. "All we want is to live on friendly terms with you; we do not want an inch of your soil; we feel sorry for you that you should be forced to fight this war for England against your will. And don't forget, Frenchmen, *England will, as before, fight to the last Frenchman.*"

And then came that never-to-be-forgotten day, the anniversary of which will fall one week from to-day—May 10th, 1940. First Holland—who had felt safe because of a comparatively recently signed treaty of non-aggression with her powerful neighbour. Then Belgium and Luxembourg, who had remained neutral for the same reason. Then France, who had very gravely, very consciously declared war on Germany, after the violation of Poland, because she had pledged her word to do so. France felt safe, however. There was the Maginot line, there was her army that had been victorious in 1918 and would, without any doubt, be victorious again.

Already, before France was actually invaded, the tragic spectacle of fleeing civilians had begun. From the smaller countries—Holland, Belgium and Luxembourg, came streams of terrified people, in cars, on bicycles, in trucks, afoot, any way, just so they might escape. Soon the inhabitants of northern France, then of the Paris region added their terror to that of their neighbours. Many told tragic tales of having been fired on by machine-guns from low-flying aeroplanes. One Belgian group, from a border village, told of families having gone to the village school at lunch-time to fetch their children, only to learn that they had been herded directly from school by the invaders into Germany, there to be brought up as Germans. Many families became separated as a result of the incredible confusion that reigned everywhere. For months the French newspapers devoted entire pages to advertisements of members of the same family who had lost each other during the flight. And the thousands of lost children—some, alas, picked up beside the bodies of mothers who had been killed by bombing! Even now, a year later, many of these children are still in the custody of public or private charitable agencies; their families have never been found.

And two weeks previous to this nightmare spectacle, France, Belgium, Holland and Luxembourg had been happy, peace-loving nations, who went about their own way, living a life they had fashioned for themselves, according to their own notions of happiness, in a land they felt was their own!

Since these fateful days, we have seen the same terrifying spectacle in other countries—in Greece, in Jugoslavia. We have seen thousands of civilians killed by bombs, others wounded or homeless in Great Britain. We look; it is certainly the ugliest sight we have ever witnessed and, as our eyes turn back to our own continent we are apt to be a bit smug and complacent as to why there is no such sight over here.

But Americans, there could be such a sight over here, despite what Colonel Lindbergh, or any other friend of Hitlerism, may say to lull you into believing the contrary. (By the way, did you ever hear Colonel—or shouldn't we now call him Herr Doktor Lindbergh?—say an unkind word about the Nazis? I never did, and I should feel vastly more reassured about his Americanism if some such word from his pen could be shown me).

We have seen in Europe the results of jay-walking and credulity in the face of heavily armed gangsterism. And if we, here in America, are worthy to survive as a free people, what must we do about it? There can be only one answer, and that is the answer that we have already given to gangsterism in our own country.

We must become not only as strong, but stronger than they are; and fight, yes fight, Americans, for the freedom that is the life-breath of this country.

Like the French, we are a peace-loving people. We are even a people who is loathe to believe in the existence of Evil, in brutality—for we have consistently tried to educate our children along this line of conduct. I don't believe that it is an exaggeration to say that most of Western Europe has shared, for many years, this love of peace which so characterises our own people. But in eastern Europe there remained an ambitious, only half-Christianised group of people that did not share it, to whom we are just weaklings to be destroyed because we feel that way.

There can be no other answer to their force but force. And just now America is the last country whose force can really count in the tragic balance between gangsterism and human freedom.

Americans, awake!

There is no time to lose. We have a great leader who has understood. Let us give him our loyalty, let us stand behind him, every man, woman and child of us in these critical days of 1941. No force on earth can conquer us if each one of us understands that *we must fight*.

Radio Address, Memorial Day 1941

MEMORIAL DAY
Broadcast
Station WNCW (Brooklyn)
May 30, 1941

To all those who, like myself, were in France on May 30th of last year, I think this Memorial Day must have a very specially poignant significance. On this date a year ago the flight of the terrified civilian populations had already begun in France, one of the most highly civilised peoples of all times had already taken to the open road, the field and the forest in order to escape the on-rush of barbarian hordes from the East. The situation in itself was not a new one in the history of Europe. But what was new was that the scientific-industrial revolution had given to the barbarians such enormous, brute strength that such elements as valour and determination to defend the Fatherland were of no avail whatsoever. It was no longer a combat of man against man, but of man against the machine. For the first time since the Thirty Years War, more civilians than soldiers were killed, and the toll for France alone—I quote recently published figures—was 180,000. Let us add to this the figure of the number of soldiers who were killed—between 90 and 100 thousand; the figure of those taken prisoner—two million—and it will give some notion of the price that France alone paid, only to end by being forced to accept a crushing defeat, a defeat that has left her sweltering in grief and bitterness, under the diabolical oppression of the victor.

As I recall all these things to-day, I remember rows on rows of little white wooden crosses that mark the graves of American lads who gave their lives twenty odd years ago in order that this thing should not happen. Have we kept faith with all those young Americans who have mingled their dust with the soil of France, under the little white crosses?

In all sincerity, I fear that we have not.

When the last taps was sounded over their graves, we withdrew completely from the dramatic discussions that followed. We watched an American president construct a possible instrument for settling all future quarrels of this kind and then, when he returned to this country, we turned our backs on his work, we disowned any responsibility to back up the victory that the boys under the crosses had paid for with their lives. I believe that there are many of us Americans who feel that, in taking this stand, we condemned Europe to the bloody second act of the drama which started in 1914 and which, if we had stood by, as we should have, need not have taken place. We were the strong, the rich, the powerful people whose resources and man power were left practically intact after the victory of 1918. In our hearts there was little ineradicable bitterness. We could have made our weight felt in all matters that concerned the organisation of the peace, just as we had done in the conclusion of the war. But we turned our backs, we did not keep faith with those who had died.

And now, in 1941, we have the opportunity to repair this great, this selfish error that we made in 1919. Are we aware of the significance of the days that lie just ahead of us now? A century ago an intense, decisive period of history was given the name of "the hundred days." I believe that we stand to-day before the most dramatic "hundred days" that has occurred since that time. June, July, August 1941—these are the hundred days that will decide whether the forces of barbarism and slavery will or will not finally dominate the world. With the incredibly courageous British, there exist silent, determined, incorruptible masses in France—with those of Belgium, Holland, Norway, Denmark, Poland, Czecho-Slovakia, Yougo-Slavia and Greece—all those suffering, silent people whose fate calls out to us as their last hope of liberation—we now have the opportunity, during the next three months, to fight the greatest fight of all times.

Let us not falter. Our President has spoken. To refuse him our support to-day is to give aid and comfort to the enemy. Let each one of us examine gravely his own conscience, give of his own strength and passion in order that, even though we did not do so twenty years ago, we may right that wrong and keep the faith to-day with the men under the white crosses.

Radio Address, July 4, 1941

Broadcast
W.C.N.W.
July 4, 1944

When I was a child, in Louisville, Kentucky, "Fourth of July," was, for me, one word, a word which, like Christmas, signified a day, of excitement and happiness that started early and only ended with a sleepy head on a welcome pillow.

Already, the evening before, a large flag hung from our front porch. The morning hours, after the official parade, were filled with a sense of general well-being punctuated with delighted terror at the cap-pistols and other noise-making fireworks the boys in our neighbourhood fired off as frequently and continuously as their savings permitted. At mid-day there was generally a family picnic and the afternoon wore off in a haze of singing and story-telling, wading in a cooling creek, watermelon, pop-corn—all those homely things that we Americans have come to associate with this day we love.

Finally, all too slowly, twilight fell. As the first fire-flies lighted up, excited preparations for the event of the day began. Both Father and Mother took part in these preparations. A long table was laid in the yard, lanterns hung from the porch and trees and, as the darkness deepened, our front yard became a fantastic place of swirling pin-wheels, star-shooting roman-candles, liquid fountains of light and sky-rockets that shot high above the trees before they burst into glory. The sounds, the smells, the beautiful fiery sights of those miraculous evenings will stay with me always; the Fourth of July has never quite lost, for me, that element of magic which, once it is implanted in a child's mind, can not be uprooted.

As I grew older, I learned of the political and human significance of this date—to the parades and fire-works were added homage to the flag; the resonant words, Liberty and Independence, a sense of solemnity, were added to the magic of those luminous childhood impressions. But I know now, that it was not until the summer of 1940 that I understood the full meaning of that July celebration. Let me explain.

In the summer of 1940 I watched our sister Republic—France—lose her independence. First, there was the 17th of June, then the Maréchal Pétain took, what Churchill termed, his melancholy decision to ask for an armistice. A week passed during which time the enemy continued to advance, all resistance having crumbled, and, on June 24th, the incredible armistice terms were announced to a stunned people. I listened to that broadcast in a French village, just on the border of the cruel German dividing line. With me were two French women; one a widow whose only son had not been heard from since May 1st, the other a young woman, the fate of whose husband was equally uncertain. I shall never forget the cry of pain uttered by these women as the terrible fate of the prisoners became known. "Our men!" fairly shrieked the younger woman, and the Mother was as though turned to stone.

The French equivalent of our July fourth was the holiday of July 14th. It was a day of national rejoicing with fireworks, lanterns, music, parades—all the same simple pleasures that we know here—set aside to celebrate the winning of French liberties, just a few years after we in this country had won ours. For many years —21 to be exact—I had taken part in these ceremonies and, in fact, the similarity of date and significance had gradually led me to think of the two holidays almost as one.

Then came July 14th 1940. Before the village monument to the dead of World War I, there was a grim, heart-rending ceremony. Soldiers of a defeated army, several hundred of them, perhaps, came before their officers to receive medals for bravery in the war they had just lost. Their uniforms were forlorn enough, but their faces were the saddest I have ever seen, in each one was reflected the image of the two million prisoners, the nearly two hundred thousand dead, the fatherland cut in two, the ruins still smoking, the ten million homeless civilians. The men fell into place to the beat of a drum, they marched away to the drum when the ceremony was finished. The villagers looked on in silence. On July 14th 1940 there were no lanterns; there was no music, no fire-works, no dancing —nothing to recall the beloved date. French Liberty was dead.

And suddenly, just as when death, for the first time, deprives us of some one dear to us we cry out; "So that is what suffering really means! That is death!" So here I knew, that I had understood fully for the first time, the real significance of the word "liberty"—now that I had watched a great people lose its liberty.

Fellow-Americans: Since 1936, we have now watched nearly twenty national units lose their liberty to a ruthless tyrant, simply because they did not understand that they must *unite* to defend it. Is there still one among us to-day who has not finally understood that our own, American, liberties are also menaced in no uncertain way, *unless we unite?* Germany's ambitions are boundless and her force is backed up with completely unscrupulous cynicism. This afternoon, when we have listened to the message of our President and read together the oath to the flag, let us turn to <u>Mein Kampf</u>, the Bible of Hitlerism. Let us ponder deeply, in the light of to-day's events such statements as these.

If we are to survive as a free people, July fourth 1941 must mark the dividing line—for many years to come until Hitlerism is beaten, in other words— between the time when this day was a rite linked simply to the past, and the dynamic, difficult years that lie ahead of us, whether we will or no.

Address to the Women's International Exhibition, November 1943

Ladies and Gentlemen:

After the Allied landing in North Africa, when Hitler occupied all of France, you will recall that our Government broke off diplomatic relations with the Vichy government of the aged Marshall Petain and invited the Vichy ambassador to spend the rest of the war in a very comfortable hotel, far from Washington. That Ambassador is still in his new quarters and it is more than probable that he will be there until the Victory bells begin to ring. And so it happened that; for the first time in the long history of friendship between our two countries—a friendship that dates from our own Revolution—there was no official French Ambassador in this country.

Soon after this sad event, however, came the most representative and the most ingratiating of Ambassadors, hundreds of them, in fact, and the American people lost no time in taking them to their hearts. These new Ambassadors were not dressed in long-tailed coats, nor did they wear diplomatic decorations on spotless evening shirts. Indeed, they were very simply dressed in the uniform of the French Navy—a dark blue sailor suit with a clean blue linen collar and on their heads a little round hat with a red wool pom-pom. Some even wore no distinguishing uniform other than the determined, weather-beaten French faces. They were nonetheless recognisable. These were the men of the French merchant marine, men who have never stopped fighting the battle of the submarine in order that urgently needed material might be carried to the Allied armies abroad. Later came soldiers and sailors who had escaped from the French islands of Guadeloupe and Martinique; commandos and aviators from England or North Africa; men from the French possessions in the South Pacific. All have constituted informal ambassadors of France in our midst, ambassadors with whom each of us has been able to talk freely and frankly. Theirs has indeed been a mission of good will.

Perhaps you will recall, if you have kept up with events that touch on France, the little flurry of excitement that ran through the population of New York— particularly the feminine population, which lost no time in copying the little hat with the red pom-pom—when French boats, after two years of absence, first reappeared in our ports. The old friendship between our two countries was once more in evidence and on every side invitations were extended by Americans of French extraction, by French men and women in exile or by American friends of France to these representatives on our soil of the suffering people from whom we were so cruelly separated.

It was out of this desire to touch their hands once more, this desire to make the French fighting man feel at home in a strange land, that the Cantine La Marseillaise was born, and it is the story of its coming into being, followed by a most informal glimpse of the daily life of the Cantine that we want to present to you this evening.

❖ ❖ ❖

We were not many, just a handful of men and women, who were determined to show these French service men that they were warmly welcome in New York. Through the generosity of that oldest of Fighting French organisations in this country, France Forever—you will recall that it was founded immediately after the fall of France, in the summer of 1940, in answer to the call for resistance of General de Gaulle—a modest nest-egg was made available. The Fighting French Veterans of the last war offered their services, as did also the women of their Auxiliary. The French-American Club lent its benediction to the project, a number of friends and patriotic citizens increased the nest-egg and Presto! the project was under way. Since, the Fighting French Relief has generously assumed a share in our running expenses, which is a great help to us.

It did not take long, for there was a magnificent spirit of cooperation among all those who were interested in seeing this idea become reality, and through the magic of love and hope two empty Second Avenue shops were soon turned into a gay French cafe; on April 17th 1943 the Cantine La Marseillaise opened its doors.

Just here I should say that we had chosen the name of our Canteen even before we chose the place, for La Marseillaise has been a rallying call to Frenchmen since 1789, and in these dark days it has become even more than before, a flaming symbol of the love of liberty that so characterizes France among the nations. For let us not forget that it was the people of France who gave us our statue of Liberty, it was the philosophers of France who influenced our ancestors to feel that without liberty death itself were better.

❖ ❖ ❖

But let us return to La Marseillaise.

You have probably already noticed an impatient group of young people waiting to come onto the stage. While they are setting the scene, I should like to tell you just a little bit more about ourselves.

Our address is 789 Second Avenue, between 42nd and 43d Streets. We are open from three o'clock until midnight every day; we have nothing to sell, everything is free to the men—all drinks, sandwiches, cakes, etc. We dance every evening and, in fact, many American and other United Nations service men come to see us to take part in our informal parties. We have some over 400 registered junior and senior hostesses. We have now welcomed many thousands of French service men, passing through New York.

Ladies and Gentlemen,—La Marseillaise!

Paris Letters from
Maria Jolas to Eugene Jolas,
September 15–October 1, 1946
(excerpts)

To: INS
From: Maria Jolas
　　3 Place Paul Painlevé 5e
Attention: Eugene Jolas
　　Bad Nauheim
Sept 15, 1946

Taking advantage of one of the rare spells of seasonable weather that this chilly end-of-summer has afforded, Monsieur Bidault's government invited all the members of the Peace Conference—including the visiting press—to a late afternoon reception which took place Wednesday at the Palace of Versailles. This brilliant event has been widely commented both informally and in the press but none has succeeded in re-creating it more successfully than the anonymous "Figaro" columnist, Guermantes, whose Sunday article under the general title of "Moments and Faces" was entirely devoted to "Versailles Day." "The reception took place in the Hall of Mirrors," he wrote, "each mirror and each one of the seventeen arcades of which was guarded by a domestic in white wig and knee breeches. On the floor were carpets [woven in] the *Savonnerie,* and in the salon known as the '*Salon de la Guerre*' a small orchestra distracted the attention of the guests from the haughty portraits which, according to Saint-Simon, made so many enemies for Louis XIVth. In the '*Salon de la Paix,*' on the contrary, there were a number of comfortable chairs from which it was possible to contemplate a horizon of lagoons and playing fountains, formal flower-beds and statues, bathed in a light of exquisite softness. During a long twilight the sun, which was reflected in the facades, played on the window-panes, re-kindled the lustreless mirrors and cast a ray of real peace over the world. Monsieur and Madame Georges

Bidault received over two thousand persons in an atmosphere of ceremonial whose pomp in no way chilled its courtesy. Then darkness began to fall. The Hall of Mirrors and the park suddenly lighted up with a poetry that was different from that of day. Night spread a peace of gleaming shadows over the reception."

A few days earlier, also in Versailles, quite as earnest if more modest seekers after peace, the Protestant Alliance of Youth Movements, had held its preliminary ecumenical studies in preparation of the ecumenical congress to be held in Oslo in 1947. Present in Versailles were 225 representatives of five protestant youth movements among whom were 60 foreigners representing 15 different nations. The theme of the Congress—"Jesus Christ, the only possible means for men to come together"—was the basis of earnest deliberations seeking an understanding among Christians that might do away with all existing divisions.

Another congress of the week was that of the Trotzsky internationalist communist group which held its first public meeting in Paris with an attendance of 100 delegates. A resolution was adopted expressing satisfaction at "the development of revolutionary tendencies in the labor unions." Satisfaction was also expressed over the addition to their ranks of "numerous militants who formerly belonged to the French Communist Party."

Mention should be made of the fact that around one thousand engineers and other technicians from every part of the world have been gathering in Paris this past week in preparation for the International Technical Congress to be held from September 16th to 21st. The problem of the possible effects of the utilization of atomic energy on existing techniques heads the agenda of this congress.

A pilgrimage organized at Lourdes especially for former prisoners and deportees and which began September 8th, attracted some 100,000 person and according to all accounts constituted a uniquely moving experience. Among the pilgrims was General Giraud, and it was in the presence of Cardinals Suhard and Saliege that 17 priests, themselves former prisoners, and Monseignor Piguet, Bishop of Clermont-Ferrand and a Dachau deportee, celebrated high mass in the open air. The Reverend Father Riquet, famous Lenten preacher of Notre Dame de Paris, urged his fellow deportees not to leave Lourdes without the firm resolution to devote themselves energetically to activities that would bring about a state of affairs whereby "in their homes, in their country, and in the world, love might triumph over hatred."

Marking the eleventh anniversary of the death of Henri Barbusse, author of Le Feu, several hundred persons representing numerous delegations gathered on Sunday at his grave in Père-Lachaise cemetery. The same day, at Villeroy, near Meaux, a number of prominent persons in civilian and military circles visited the grave of the poet Charles Peguy, author of the Mystère de Jeanne d'Arc. And in Maillance, in Provence, a numerous gathering celebrated the 116th anniversary of the birth of the poet Frederic Mistral, author of <u>Mireille</u>.

❖ ❖ ❖

In Geneva a number of French writers, among them, Julien Benda and Jean Guéhenno, are participating in the discussion taking place in connection with the program entitled "Rencontres Internationales" organized by a committee of eminent Swiss professors, artists and other intellectuals around the theme: the "European Spirit." The Parisian public has been kept informed of these deliberations through the press and the radio and on Friday evening a round-table radio programme in the French language grouped Benda and Guehenno with the Swiss writer Denis de Rougemont, the English poet Stephen Spender and some three or four other participants of different nationalities. Various suggestions for attaining European unity were put forward. Spender felt a degree of abandon of national sovereignty would be inevitable. To this de Rougemont replied that he was himself not at all clear as to the exact steps to be taken and felt that if writers everywhere would lay down their pens until the reading public and recovered from its present state of mental and moral indigestion, M. Guéhenno replied that, in reality, European writers might as well have been silent for the last forty years as they had written without belief in anything. Discussing these meetings in <u>Le Figaro</u> of September 13th, Monsieur Guéhenno, who is professor at the Ecole Normale Supérieure and toured South America in 1945 on a cultural mission for his country, wrote as follows: "Nothing could be more vain and more dangerous perhaps than a European nationalism. . . . From now on the European spirit should give strength to the organization of the United Nations, and it is only within the framework of that organization that the historical juncture will one day be able to create the entity Europe. The time has come when the European nations, all of them equally poor, can finally reach a political and intellectual understanding and together serve in the development of the will to attack a truth that is both critical and just and which is the very basis of the European spirit."

Translations of books by Henry Miller, author of <u>Tropic of Cancer</u> and <u>Black Spring</u>, having been the object of a complaint on the part of the "Cartel of Moral and Social Action" which seeks to ban them on the grounds of obscenity, the weekly newspaper <u>Carrefour</u> questioned several French writers on the subject of this ban. Jean Cocteau, according to the author of the *enquête,* simply threw his hands in the air and declared that the whole affair smacked of the Middle Ages about which he knew nothing. Francis Carco used four favorite Parisian adjectives: "Grotesque! Ridiculous! Odious! Abominable!" He added that he considered Miller was the victim of Jean-Paul Sartre and that he, Carco, was doing all in his power to help Miller to come to Paris and take his own defense. Questioned on the subject, Sartre's first comment was, "Stupide!" He then added that he did not much care for Miller's work, which he found overdone, but at that at least Miller was not trying to make money through the use of obscenity, it was just his conception of the world.

Under the title, "At the Cradle of Tomorrow's Literature," Paul Guth has just published two articles in Le Littéraire describing an evening spent with each of two groups of very young poets now emerging in Paris: the "Pentacle," whose "pope," François Chevais, is only five years from his baccalauréat de 'philo' at the Lycée Henri Quatre, and the "Sensorialists" whose chef d'école is Jean Legrand.

Among the members, both masculine and feminine, of the "Pentacle," there is, according to Guth, a tendency to "remove their hats six times for each letter in his name " at the mention of the former Surrealist poet, Paul Eluard. Otherwise, their admiration goes to such of their elders as Marcel Aymé, Prévert, Breffort, Cendrars, Michaux; they consider themselves more sur-real than surrealiste and have a decided taste for the neologism. In his off time, Chevais is also a painter and the circle is the sign he has chosen to represent the "absurd."

As for the "Sensorialists," theirs would appear to be a more enveloping philosophy with literature constituting only one of its many manifestations. They want not only to "restore to our epoch a sense of love," for they consider that "the real basis of all friendship is not intellectual but affective," but they also have evolved a system of diet that, at first glance, seems to be quite sound even from the standpoint of the nutritionists. Upon examination; however, we find that for them milk, sugar, bread and almonds are consumed with a view to increasing gentleness, energy, sincerity and morale rather than proteins, carbo-hydrates and vitamins. It would be interesting too to know the results of the sensorial experiments —(could these be former pupils of the Dottoressa Montessori?) which take place in the Chamber of Fruits, the Chamber of Woven Goods, the Chamber of Odors and the Chamber of Modesty. But, according to Legrand, it has all been told in his book; Journal de Jacques, published by Gallimard, after a previous book, his own preference, entitled Jacques l'Homme Possible, had been turned down by all publishers.

Among the latest magazines, Esprit devotes its entire number just out this week, to an enquête on the "gulf between the Christian and the modern worlds." How did it form? What do you suggest as a solution for bridging it and what do you think of those already proposed? "Among the many replies chosen by the editor Emmanuel Mounier—replies from Julien Benda, Louis Hadamard, François Mauriac, Denis de Rougemont and others—that of the Russian philosopher, Nicolas Berdaieff, long a resident of Paris, is particularly interesting. Berdaieff considers that the "historical forms of Christianity which lived off the fading light of the past are outmoded, and Christianity of all sects is weak in the presence of what is taking place in the world today." He adds that only a conversion of Christianity towards the light that emanates from the future will be able to restore its creative power. For this, he feels that not only a modification of the conscience within the heart of Christendom will be necessary, but that also the attitude of Christianity towards a movement as powerful as communism—"which contains both a Christian truth and poison"—will have to be modified. Berdaieff considers that this "poison" is due to the sins of the Christians.

September 23, 1946

The event of the week, of course, was the interview given by General de Gaulle to the French Press Agency in which he declared that he would give his blessing to any political party that opposed the constitution now under discussion in favor of that outlined by him in his Bayeux speech. Reactions varied from the cry of alarm of Pierre Hervé in <u>L'Humanité</u> (Communist), who urged all republicans to "unite against the threat to their liberties constituted by the activities of the candidate for presidential dictatorship," to the declaration of the Minister of War, M. Michelet (M.R.P.) who, speaking at Tulle, reminded his hearers that "before he became the hero of the 18th of June, de Gaulle was the author of a clairvoyant report dated January 1940." M. Michelet added that in his opinion it was "inconceivable that the liberator of the country should not be free to offer whatever advice he felt the occasion demanded." In general, however, it was probably a little paragraph in <u>Gavroche</u> (Socialist) which more nearly expressed the reaction of the majority of the population. Under the title: "Is de Gaulle a Gaullist?" an anonymous columnist wrote: "If we are to believe Remy de Gourmont, Machiavelli was the least machiavellic of men. Is the General a Gaullist? Or, at any rate, is he behind the 'Gaullist Union'? 'That is the question,' as the English say. And there are many who would like to be certain about this point in order to determine their action in the coming elections." There is no doubt that the personality of M. René Capitant—a figure from the more fiery works of Alexander Dumas père—has served only too well the enemies of the 'Gaullist Union,' of which he is president and principal animator.

Rémy Roure, writing in <u>Une Semaine dans le Monde</u> on the "Resistance" strikes a note of melancholy and warning as he points out the increasingly negative character of its rôle in French life to-day, just two years after the liberation. Although it is constantly being evoked at commemorative ceremonies, M. Roure compares these evocations to those of a ghost.

"The Resistance itself," he writes, "wrapped in a purple shroud. Can it rise again? . . . Did it accomplish its task at the moment of Liberation? Perhaps so. But we do not believe it. It is impossible that this great hope should have vanished. When men and parties make use of it for their personal interests, this is nevertheless a tribute, for they recognize its inner force . . . The worst that could happen no doubt would be that it should be evoked by those who violently opposed it in its radiant clandestinity, by those who were its detractors and occasionally its executioners, and who sought its protection when it triumphed. Worse still would be if it should become the source of civil discord, if, after having united the best among Frenchmen, it should turn one against the other. There is still time to avoid such a tragic eventuality."

In the Palais Bourbon the debates around the new constitution lead far afield, in an attempt to formulate the future status of Overseas-France in its relationship to the Metropolis. In an impassioned plea for a more liberal policy towards the 64 millions that constitute the population of the French Empire, the poet-deputy from Martinique, Aimé Césaire recalled that France had signed the Charter of the United Nations, which repudiated colonialism. "France cannot therefore, turn backward; this would be a denial before the whole world. Colonialism is also contrary to the principles of the social and democratic Republic which France has decided to build. There is no question of disavowing what France has already accomplished. The French conscience has always condemned the practise of a certain type of "colonialism" against which Gallieni himself protested, as did also the great man of years and wisdom that was Montaigne. . . . Slavery was never a mile-stone on the road to liberty!" cried Césaire, and he was warmly applauded. Césaire recalled abuses in the recent past which led to expropriations, forced labor and other forms of exploitation. "France must transform this régime," he declared, "and lead the over-seas' populations to democracy." "More is asked of them than is given them," he concluded, "and since in time of war we speak of 'Senegalese sharp-shooters' why in times of peace should we not speak of 'African Democracy'?"

Under the title: "The Destiny of the Empire is that of France" Jean Griot examined the problem in Le Figaro. Pointing out that the Fourth Republic would not have the facilities for constituting an Empire that had been enjoyed by the Third Republic, Monsieur Griot warned that the Constitution proposed last June had carried with it rather the dangers of disintegration than the possibilities of association. In an attempt to find a solution, he quoted the president of the Radical-Socialist Party M. Edouard Herriot who urged recently that the Soviet Constitution be studied as an example. Herriot pointed out however that the Russian problem had been an easier one due to the fact that the peoples in question were juxtaposed, whereas the French problem demanded a solution that would unite peoples dispersed throughout the world to the metropolis. "The Russian Constitution," said M. Herriot, "has the virtue of first defining the federating organ." The problem, in other words, is "to define with precision the powers of the federating organism and those of the colonies." And Herriot added: "This is just plain common sense."

A short bus-ride from the scene of these discussions the Peace Conference of the twenty-one nations continues its toilsome not to say tedious existence and, as the weeks wear on, the Parisian public would seem to become more and more disenchanted with the spectacle. In the Littéraire, the chronicler who signs "Grippe-Soleil" does not hide his weariness. "One must be a good sailor," he writes, to be able to navigate through the salons of the phantom vessel which the Luxembourg Palace has become since the Paris Conference took it over. Absurd novels à la Kafka unfold their vertiginous time-marking in the different commission rooms. In one room it takes three quarters of an hour to decide whether or not each delegate shall be limited to a fifteen minute speech. In another, there is a mournfully tenacious discussion to decide whether such and such an amendment shall be put to a vote. And when, depressed to the point of nausea, I succeed in escaping, I am pursued from corridor to corridor, even to that last refuge, the bar, by the cavernous, pitiless voices of the loud speakers which spare no subtlety in all the languages of the world. The up-rooted Tower of Babel, like a drunken ship, is sinking slowly to the bottom of the oceans of absurdity."

Under the title: "Academism and Public Good," Georges Duhamel writing in Le Figaro expresses the same scepticism. "I place no hope in the deliberations of these assemblies," he writes, "which are the mass and religious services of our unhappy modern society. Do I dare add that I do not believe in what is called the work of assemblies and congresses? . . . I believe in the work of a man working alone; a man who has weighed everything, constructed, corrected and finally signed everything that is done. All the rest is stuff and nonsense."

However, the possible results of this "time-marking" for France, have not passed un-noticed and it is with real disquiet that certain observers analyse the situation. "Between two Bogs" is the title of an unsigned editorial in Sunday's Semaine dans le Monde, the weekly supplement of the newspaper, Le Monde: "France is, in reality, between two bogs. On one side, as on the other, if she should dare to advance she would risk being swallowed up. She is not, she is no longer, on an equal footing with the new empires, and they have no need of her either to reach an accord or to fight each other. If she tried to mix in the complicated game of their interests, the best she would get out of it would be to be the first victim of their conflict—or of their understanding. Faced with this impossible choice, shall she refuse to go forward, which is what she has done for several months?" The author concludes that this cannot be the line France must choose, but on the contrary, she must take a courageous line, straight ahead, which is the "line of international justice, even at the price of neutrality." He advises that to remain aloof from politics is today the best policy for France, that she has little to lose and much to gain. Under the title: "Facing the Soviet Problem," Pierre Bourdan, Le Figaro editorialist, writes: "Whether or not she is able to make herself heard, the rôle of France is to speak with the voice of reason, to dare to open in broad daylight the dossiers of great Empires, to ask for definitions, to throw light on intentions, to provoke examination of what is just or unjust, of what is possible and what is dangerous. What if this is a pretentious rôle? It is justified by the threat that hangs over her due to a rivalry which could result in Europe being seized and crushed."

The French reactions, especially among the Catholic groups, to the recently announced attempt on the part of the Soviet Government to "mobilize the spirit in the service of the socialist fatherland" have not been lacking. François Mauriac, citing the passage in the declaration made by the Soviet Writers' Union, condemning "mistaken political tendencies and a spirit of indifference to political matters," observes that "the crime of indifference has never yet been punished in any known religion. Stanislas Fumet, writing in the Catholic leftist weekly Le Temps Présent, goes more deeply into the problem. "We might ask," he says, "if art can remain free when life is not free. I fear that with the success of materialism, we shall have to progressively renounce this freedom. The French communists were badly advised the day they opened their doors to Picasso. Soon they will have to send him back to the Trotzkyists or to the anarchists of his native country."

The establishment in Paris of the cultural services of the United Nations Organization—"Unesco"—is a source of satisfaction to the French press. They have taken note that the plan of the new organization is a more inclusive one than that of the former, "Institute of intellectual Cooperation" and there is hardly a publication which has not given a detailed account of the opening of the new offices in the Hotel Majestic under the direction of Julian Huxley. The French Government's permanent representative in the preparatory commission is M. Julien Cain, general administrator of the Bibliothèque Nationale, and the committee of experts includes such names as Henri Wallon, education, Pierre Auger, higher scientific instruction, Lucien Febure, social sciences, Jean Cassou, arts, Jean Painlevé, scientific and educational cinema, Vladimir Porché, radio, Eve Curie, press, etc. Henri Laugier, well-known scientist, former head of cultural services in the Provisional Government and now a French representative to the United Nations Organization, has just been replaced by Louis Joxe as Director General of Cultural

Relations in the Foreign Ministry. M. Joxe, who was closely associated with Professor Laugier already in the Algiers government, is the youngest member of the Conseil d'Etat and his nomination to his new post has been cordially commented upon on all sides.

Whether there is any truth in the rumor or not cannot yet be confirmed, but the communist daily "Humanité" published a short note to the effect that Jean-Paul Sartre is considering opening his own "Existentialist" Institute with his co-editors at Les Temps Modernes, Merleau-Ponty, Robert Aron and Mme. Simone de Beauvoir as leading members of the teaching staff.

A literary event of the week was the death of Bernard Groethuysen, who died in Luxembourg where he had gone for a vacation. Groethuysen was the author of a Histoire de la philosophie allemande depuis Nietzsche which has become a classic. It was also Groethuysen who introduced such writers as Kafka and Kierkegaard to France.

The appearance of André Gide's Thésée has been hailed by many as the literary testament of the author of the Symphonie Pastorale—which has just met with such great success in the cinema version shown for the first time at the Cannes Cinema Festival. According to Robert Kemp, writing in the Nouvelles Littéraires, Thésée is not one of the more profound of Gide's works. Kemp sees in it rather a sort of review of Gide's favorite themes, "only less provoking, less sharp and penetrating than they were originally." Kemp also finds the themes bathed "in a sort of unctious wisdom which comes to us all as evening falls." Louis Parrot, reviewing Thésée in Les Lettres Françaises, finds that this "patiently constructed work " is the prey of a "secret malady" i.e. a lack of faith. He adds that it is perhaps faith more than anything else which Gide has lacked. "With all his gifts, his unique style, veiled by his sensibility and irony, his immense culture, Andre Gidé could have done much more than he has done," is the conclusion of this critic.

The weekly Gavroche picks up an echo from the Tribune de Genève according to which forty thousand unpublished verses by Arthur Rimbaud, author of the "Bateau Ivre," have been discovered in Addis-Ababa. Although extremely sceptical as to the accuracy of this announcement the author of the article, Fernand Lot, urges Jean Paulhan "if it is in his power," not to leave the public languishing too long.

[October 1, 1946]

Under the title "The Future of Mankind," Jean Rostand, distinguished biologist son of the author of Cyrano do Bergerac, examines this week in Les Lettres

<u>Françaises</u> the possibility of applying the principles of scientific breeding that have been so successfully applied to plants and animals, to the amelioration of the human species. He is well aware of the fact that such a project seems not only ridiculous and distasteful to the average man but that it also contains an affront to his sense of liberty and personal dignity. There is the undeniable fact too that whereas we know what type of plant or animal we are trying to obtain, there is little unanimity of opinion as to what constitutes the human goal. Rostand considers, however, that the problem is quite as serious as that of the atomic bomb and, going even further, he speculates as to whether a humanity decimated by the discoveries of its physicists will not be reduced to asking the biologists to compensate in quality for what it has lost in quantity. In any case, Rostand declares that the power not only to change profoundly but greatly to improve the human race is ever now in the hands of the biologists. He recognizes that the social conscience of 1946, emerging from the shock of recent crudely inhuman experiments, is entirely unprepared to accept any sort of selective biological methods, and he feels the role of the scientist today should be confined to educating the public so that it will become aware of the phenomena of heredity. In conclusion he states, however, that he refuses to believe that man as such suffices for the mankind of the future.

In the same number of <u>Les Lettres Françaises</u>, Edith Thomas, whose talent as a short-story writer was revealed in the clandestine papers of the Resistance, examines the problem of the relation of man to the machine. Miss Thomas, recalling Georges Duhamel's warning as to the psychological changes humanity is undergoing due to the technical revolution, believes that there is today a noticeable atrophy of the human sentiments on which, for centuries, men had based their notions of civilization. She points out a diminishing sympathy and respect for man as exemplified in the writings of a number of well-known authors and urges her fellow writers to consciously defend the "humanist against the automat."

Approaching man's relation to science from the metaphysical angle, Robert Aron, in his most recent work, <u>Retour à l'Eternel</u>, expresses the opinion that twentieth-century science has evolved considerably in its traditional relationships with religion, and he adds that religion too has advanced remarkably. "In other words," according to Aron, " it is less opposed than was the science of the 19th century to the return of God among us." He considers that this state of affairs dates approximately from the day when Bergson introduced the notion of the unforeseeable in opposition to Claude Bernard, and he points out that more recently still, the well-known savant Professor Lapicque was heard to declare: "Life is a struggle against the laws of physics." In an interview with Aron in <u>Le Figaro</u>, he stated that a number of theologians were now trying to assimilate these two positions thus far considered to be opposed, adding that the results of these attempts were leading towards a transformation of certain points of dogma of which the Church, apparently, does not disapprove.

The author of L'Ame Romantique et le Rêve Albert Béguin, writing in the monthly review La Nef presents an interesting study on Balzac and the social classes. For Balzac, according to Béguin, society is an exciting spectacle, but in reality he is more attached to the individual character, for the staging of whose passions and gestures society is but the theatre.

Writing in the September number of Europe, Jean Larcenac contests the generally accepted opinion that Zola is a class writer, in the Marxist sense of the term, that is to say, that he has contributed to the development of revolutionary dynamism in the masses of society. Larcenac considers that there is in the works of Zola an absence of deep sympathy for his characters with whom he himself is rarely identified. According to Larcenac, too there is little indication in the works of Zola that he was aware of the obscure political activity of the working classes. In this connection it is interesting to note that the Communist daily Ce Soir published this week an important article on Zola by Francis Jourdain, who knew Zola personally. The article is illustrated by a reproduction of a portrait by Vallotton and the photostat copy of a manuscript letter from Zola thanking Jourdain for having organized a meeting in which it had been possible for him to hear the "great voice of Jaurès announcing magnificently the blessed city of to-morrow." A pilgrimage to Zola's former home in Médan, organized Sunday by the "Society of the Friends of Emile Zola" was presided by Louis Aragon.

Two new laws published this week in the Journal Officiel have brought a definite improvement in the status of the writer in France. The Constituent Assembly created on September 20th a "Caisse Nationale de Lettres" the aim of which will be "to sustain and encourage the literary activity of writers through scholarships, loans, subventions, the acquisition of books and all other means that will permit compensation of the realization of a literary work." Another law, consideration of which dates from before the war, permits the revision, twenty years later, of all condemnations "for outrage to good morals" of literary works that have become classics. It is the intention of the "Société des Gens de Lettres" to take advantage of this new ruling to obtain the rehabilitation of certain works of Baudelaire and, later, of Flaubert, which were banned at the time of publication. In this connection, the Gazette des Lettres, recalling the recent ban of Henry Miller's work, is surprised to discover blank spaces in the typographical composition of Raymond Guerin's latest book, L'Apprenti, which bear every trace of censorship, whether by a timid publisher remains to be seen.

Recent literary events include a reception in honor of the American negro writer, Richard Wright, given by the weekly Carrefour. Wright, who is the author of <u>Native Son</u> and <u>Black Boy</u> has stated his intention to settle in France indefinitely. The well-known critic Charles du Bos has just published the first volume of his <u>Journal</u> containing interviews with Bergson, Gide, Valéry and accounts of decades of the famous Pontigny gatherings that ended with the war. <u>Cahiers du Sud</u> has published a number entirely devoted to Paul Valéry which contains notes by Gide, Fargue and a number of other contemporaries of the poet of the "Cimetière Marin." Francis de Miomandre, in the <u>Nouvelles Littéraires</u>, speculates maliciously on the fact that the entire Rimbaud legend will have to be altered if the announcement made recently concerning the discovery of forty thousand hitherto unpublished verses by author of <u>Illuminations</u> should really be true.

Before going to Cannes to take part in the International Cinema Festival now in progress there, Michèle Morgan lent new glamour to the opening of the Théâtre Marignan on Friday, which might also be called the opening of the Paris season, if the brilliance of the audience is any criterion. The occasion, the first performance in Paris of the film version of André Gide's <u>Symphonie Pastorale</u>, caused "Guermantes" in <u>Le Figaro</u> to comment that "in an irritable world in which envy follows so closely upon hatred, only the Cinema retains the privilege of disarming the crowd and charming it at the same time." "Guermantes" notes that the crowd seemed perhaps more interested in Michèle Morgan, the interpreter of the film, than in André Gide, the author, but that due to the intense beauty of this French star, just back from her American triumphs, even Monsieur Gide seemed to accept this fact as quite natural.

Discussing the Cannes Festival in the <u>Nouvelles Littéraires</u> Georges Charensol expresses the opinion that although it has been extremely interesting to see the films of so many different countries, especially certain documentary films, the contributions of France and the United States have far outclassed those of the other countries represented.

Except for an exhibition of paintings by the well-known Brazilian painter, Portinari, due to open at the Galerie Charpentier on October second, there is little activity among the galeries for the moment. This does not mean, however, that the painters themselves are not active, and it is with real impatience that the Parisian theatre public is awaiting the openings of three plays for which André Masson, who returned in the autumn of 1945 after five years in the United States, has designed the décor: Armand Salacrou's <u>La Terre est Ronde</u>; André Gide's translation of <u>Hamlet</u>, with Jean-Louis Barrault in the leading rôle, and <u>Morts sans Sépulture</u>, the new play by Jean-Paul Sartre. All three of these plays are due to open in the next weeks.

The return to Paris of Ludimilla Pitoeff, after five years in the United States, is good news to all pre-war theatre goers and their curiosity is considerably aroused by the announcement that, among other rôles, she plans to play that of Racine's <u>Phèdre</u>.

The single first performance of Pierre Emmanuel's play <u>Le Lépreux</u>, which was broadcast over the National Radio, constituted an innovation on the part of the French broadcasting services which, if it pleases the public, will be followed by other first performances. Jean Gandrey-Rety, writing in the weekly newspaper <u>Arts</u>, finds <u>Le Lépreux</u> interesting if somewhat oratorical. André Warnod, on the other hand, was very favorably impressed and he wrote in <u>Le Figaro</u> that it had "a poetic quality which at times attains grandeur."

Lecture on the Songs and Tales of American Folklore, March 5, 1947

(excerpt)

I am infinitely touched by this reception, not that I take the honor for myself or even entirely for the Organisation that I represent, American aid to France, that has lived among you here in Saint-Dié all year.

No, I know there is a great interest among you in this wild country you were the first to name more than four centuries ago. You wonder what it has become? When you strangely baptized it, with such hope and confidence, France already had a long and glorious history. It was already a nation. Under the reign of François Premier, it had already had a great renascence in the arts: Ronsard, Rabelais were already writing their immortal works. And what was happening in those years on the new continent, discovered, almost by chance, by Christopher Columbus?

It was a great forest, peopled by the American Indians, some of whose legends and songs I would like to tell you about, how I understood them in my Louisville, Kentucky. [Then she tells them about Captain John Smith, about John Ohlden and Puisella, whom he loved, George Washington, Benjamin Franklin, and about the Fourth of July and the Declaration of Independence, about Thanksgiving and its turkey and cranberry sauce, about Valentine's Day, about Labor Day, and then the legends of Rubwaniskon (Rip Van Winkle), about Evangeline, and about Grandcor (Groundhog Day), before singing them some old songs. All the children wrote letters of appreciation for Maria's talk.].

Given by Maria Jolas as Directrice du Service d'Information de l'Aide Américaine á la France.

Sketch of the Years 1952–1970

Once the sorrow and rudderlessness left by Gene's lingering illness and death had abated, my widowhood fell quite naturally into three main parts: grandmother —by 1960 there were 5 grandchildren, all of whom spent their vacations with me, in Chérence; translator—of all of my dear friend Nathalie Sarraute's books as they appeared; of Gaston Bachelard's La Poétique de l'espace, and, finally, in 1970, at the request of the Beacon Press of Boston, of La Communauté étudi-ante, a historian's brilliant record of the 1968 student revolt in Paris, by Pierre Vidal-Naquet, assisted by Alain Schnapp. This latter work was a 650 page book containing many technical terms and locutions with which I was unfamiliar. Without the author's kind and constant help, I could not have made this trans-lation.

With the third phase, that of militant dissenter to the U.S. war in Vietnam— I had already noted the name of Pierre Vidal-Naquet in my address book, as a French intellectual who could be counted on to help the penniless U.S. desert-ers who were drifting into Paris, pursued by the authorities, and whom our modest group of anti-war Paris-Americans: PACS (Paris American Committee to Stop War), had undertaken to guide to safety. These were our responsibility, our "boys," and in order not to forget the name of their French friend, I noted it in my address book, under *Boys*. I had lived in ignorance of the French aca-demic world, and I did not for a moment dream that our cause could be de-fended directly and warmly by one of the leading Hellenists, a rarely gifted scholar of his time.

My translation of the French Student Uprising was published in 1971, and we, later, together—P. V-N. as he signs, has an excellent knowledge of English— made translations of some five or six of his articles on different aspects of ancient history, mainly Greek. Contact with his extraordinary erudition and the pleas-ure of reading his brilliant, never obscure prose, have opened up vistas for me of which I was totally ignorant. As the years passed, I have come to cherish most, among our male friends, platonically but deeply, my friendship with Pierre Vidal-Naquet.

I should add that I shall soon be ninety years old, while Pierre is a brilliant 52, with an admirable wife and three grown sons, the eldest of whom, Denis, is also an attentive, intelligent friend to me. Life does, sometimes, have its compensations.

End-dream, August 1975

Along with a number of scholarly words that occasionally cropped up in my reading during the Louisville years, which I am tempted to call unidimensional, the word "eschatology" remained for a long time in the limbo of words that I read without investigating their full meaning. And yet those years were not entirely unidimensional: the shaft that should have led to deeper knowledge had two of the required dimensions. But it was a shallow shaft, excavation had long been abandoned at a level that presented no resistance; we could still breathe comfortably, still pursue our light-hearted scheme of things undisturbed by questioning; life was life, death was death, these were mysteries; mercifully, religion had long since assumed them both, which left us free to concentrate on matters more directly our concern.[47] Eschatology, then, had inspired little curiosity, not enough in any case, for me to have made it a part of my own thinking, and this in spite of the fact that when, in 1919, I left America for France, the French people's most recent plunge into an era of mass death had left a visible trail of mourning and loss; most of the women were dressed in black, many men were wearing black arm-bands. But even transplanted into a world of distress, my own confidence in *this* life never faltered, and as for the life to come, it could wait.

As the years passed, deaths occurred that caused me deep grief: my younger brother Angus, my beloved father, our ill-starred baby, the Nazi massacres, Joyce . . . but I do not recall seeking comfort or wisdom beyond my own capacity to bear pain; my early religious teachings had paled in oblivion.

In 1952, however, when I saw the word "Eschatology" written in Gene's large, well-formed handwriting on a folder into which he had been slipping poems

---

47. Actually, no forest tribe was ever more absorbed in its own affairs, more unconcerned with the outside world. Its great virtue: it was an amiable tribe, its members were generally kind to one another and hospitable to (white) strangers. It possessed a well-structured, tolerant code of conduct for "its own kind" and a diversified tradition of pleasures, both formal and informal. Boredom was unknown.

and other jottings, I understood; I knew now that for each individual, in addition to knowledge of age-old beliefs, it opened up an existential approach to personal annihilation, that it was also a vessel into which one could pour one's own doubts and hopes.

Gene had been ill for many months, he was dying; he was aware of this, we both were, yet somehow, out of *pudeur* (the English language lacks this word), we could not speak of it together. To my sorrow, I fear that the folder marked "Eschatology" may have been the closest confidant of his fears during those last months of apprehensive certainty. The profound pessimism of the Schopenhauerian reflexions that had all but replaced his traditional Lorraine upbringing, the sum of tragedy and suffering that this geographical servitude entailed had left him, I believe, little respite from eschatological preoccupations. And yet when, at the end, as long promised, I arranged for him to be given the Catholic sacrament of extreme unction, his look of terror as, roused from somnolence, he gradually became aware of the priest's presence, convinced me that no article of faith, no corpus of speculations had succeeded in cushioning the sharp pain of ultimate cognition.

For many years, Gene had made a conscious effort to free himself from what he called the "diabolical principle," chief source of his permanent disagreement with the surrealists. This effort was evident in much of his writing: his admiration for the works of Novalis, of Hugo Ball, both of whom he translated; his "verticalist" then "vertigralist" experiments; his translations of Fechner, including Life after Death the very title of his own Planets and Angels; his insistence on "white" as opposed to "black" romanticism . . . were all expressions of an aspiration to transcend the diabolical, to face extinction not only without anguish, but in ecstasy. Joyce too, probably, had hoped, through his intellect, to exorcise the punitive features of his religious upbringing. Yet I recall that he could not bring himself to speak of death, and that when Transition published a memorial tribute to the German poet Elsa von Freitag Loringhoven, this was considered by him almost as an aggression. I know too that there was deep fear in that Zurich hospital room as January 13, 1941 dawned.[48]

And I, myself? What of my own death? These thoughts are not gratuitous, but have been prompted by a recent dream, a dream and not unnaturally, constant public speculation with regard to the events that will follow the death, more politely referred to as "disappearance," of Mao, Franco, Tito—to mention only these three, all of whom are my close contemporaries, (I am even a year older than Mao).

---

48. "*Vous n'avez pas peur de la mort—moi, si!*" (You do not fear death. I do!) he wrote Martha Fleischmann on Dec. 9, 1918.

End-dream 2

In my dream, I had already died, and someone, invisible, nameless, was giving the final touches to my "laying out." I saw my folded hands, resting on a long grey shroud, my colorless lips, closed eyes. I felt grateful to the person who was gently brushing my hair in preparation for its definitive arrangement. "Is it clean?" I asked myself. "Does she—he?—know how I like it combed?" Just here I awoke, the sight I had witnessed still very vivid, accompanied by no distress, however, only interest in the capacity of the dream to project so clearly and logically such an illogical scene. Borrowing from my old friend, Sam Beckett, he surely will not object, I call this experience "end-dream." But need it foretell an approaching end? Might it not reflect merely somewhat simplistic habits of thought to which has now been added the death-goal that Freud, late in life, assigned to us all. There could be more years, more dreams, before the end. And I dare to hope that this manifestation of eschatological awareness, however naïvely classical, may hold some promise of serenity. Years ago, I erected a sapling tree, in Kentucky, to mark the last resting place of the seven of us, in the hope, probably, that, if not in life, at least in death, I would "come home."

Vain provision. It is now over 55 years since I uprooted my sapling tree and brought it back to the world from which its ancestors had sprung some 200 years earlier. Its ash will mingle with the old soil. Nor does this mean that I don't often find myself humming softly "Weep no more, my lady. . . ." With affection, however, not with nostalgia.

Index